How God

Can Save Your

MARRIAGE

In 40 Days

By Alex A. Lluch

Author of Over 3 Million Books Sold!

HOW GOD CAN SAVE YOUR MARRIAGE IN 40 DAYS

BY ALEX A. LLUCH

Published by WS Publishing Group
San Diego, California 92119
Copyright © 2010 by WS Publishing Group

Designed by: David Defenbaugh, Sarah Jang, WS Publishing
Group

For inquiries:
Log on to www.WSPublishingGroup.com
E-mail info@WSPublishingGroup.com

ISBN-13: 978-1-934386-84-2

Printed in China

Table of Contents

GOD WANTS YOU TO
Save Your Marriage

Introduction

GOD WANTS YOU TO
Save Your Marriage

Hatshepsut and the Pharaoh Thutmose II were married some time in the mid-1400s B.C.E. Historians estimate the couple's arranged marriage took place when Hatshepsut was 12 and Thutmose II was 15. Thutmose II died an early death, while his bride went on to rule for 20 years in his place, as Pharaoh. It was even reported that she wore a fake beard and dressed in men's clothes to enforce her rule of law—making Hatshepsut the first female ruler of a nation in recorded history. Talk about a power couple!

Though you and your spouse may never rule the world together, you can certainly nurture your relationship into a similar state of greatness. The first step toward a resplendent marriage is to treat each other like royalty. Make him your Pharaoh, and let her be your queen. Of course, it may not be easy to give your partner the royal treatment with your relationship in its current state. But with hard work, dedication, commitment, and faith in God's Word, you will transform your troubled relationship into a holy and loving marriage.

How God Can Save Your Marriage in 40 Days offers a step-by-step guide for how to become a better partner and enrich your relationship with your spouse. In the process, you will gain insight into the ways in which your attitude, behavior, and mindset affect the quality and health of your marriage. You will be reminded of God's holy presence in your relationship through powerful Bible verses that give you a daily assignment. Let God's words fill in whenever yours fail and know that this will be a road fraught with challenges, struggles, and questions. However, the work you do will reap heavenly rewards both in your marriage and in your spiritual life.

Why 40 Days?

Forty is a significant number that appears in several verses throughout the Bible. It is most often used to signify a period of trial, such as when Jesus was tempted by the devil in the wilderness for 40 days. It also marks a new beginning, like when Jesus was resurrected for 40 days after his entombment. Similarly, in Genesis 7:12, God chooses to wash the world clean to start anew, and thus makes it rain for 40 days and 40 nights. Like these stories, your marriage has likely gone through one or more difficult trials and you are now ready for a new start. The 40 topics in this book include exercises that will help carry you through these difficult times and give new life to your relationship.

In addition to the Biblical significance, 40 days is the minimum amount of time it takes to absorb the spiritual, behavioral, and personality changes this book asks you to make. At times, your efforts will go unnoticed, un-thanked, or may be flat-out rejected. Forty days, however, is just enough time to recover from such rejection and to move beyond any setbacks. Forty days also affords you enough time to progress on to the next topic with renewed determination, because there is always another assignment to try and another chance to succeed. Your partner will come to trust your efforts when he or she notices that they continue beyond a day, a week, or even a month. At the same time, forty days allows you to establish a consistent way of conducting yourself that will soon enough become your new way of life.

How Can God Save My Marriage?

There are times when our problems loom so large, they threaten to crush us. The fear of the dissolution of a marriage is one of those times. When the negative energy in your marriage seems to take on a life of its own, it is natural to wonder, "What happened to us?" During times of great turmoil, confusion, and doubt, God offers His wisdom in the Word. Give your problems to Him in prayer to relieve your burden, and He will guide you toward answers. Of course, this does not mean God is going to appear before you in your bedroom to tell you to send your wife flowers or to stop badgering your husband to take out the trash. Rather, prayer is focused and informed meditation on a problem that opens you up to receive God's guidance through careful attention to the Word.

In addition, God gives clear instructions for how to be a good person in the Bible. Follow His instructions for holy living (such as those detailed in Colossians 3:1-17) and you will see positive results in your marriage. Certainly, it will benefit your relationship to always be kind, compassionate, and truthful with your spouse. How can you go wrong if you henceforth put love above all else and forgive your partner as God has forgiven you? These are but a few of the many ways in which turning to God for guidance can save your marriage.

What If I Am Unsure of My Faith?

The problems within your marriage likely started around the same time as your spiritual doubt. It does not matter whether your troubled relationship caused you to doubt God's love, or vice versa. When we live our lives without faith we falter in many, if not all, of the areas in our lives. We become dissatisfied with our work, our bodies, and even our marriages because we are deprived of our spiritual foundation. Without it we feel bankrupt and empty. Nothing but the restoration of our faith can fill that void—not even the love of a devoted spouse.

Most people will question, doubt, or lose their faith completely at least once in their lifetime, while others come to God's love later in life. No matter which kind of person you are, the important thing to know is that God will always welcome you back. Lamentations 3:40 consoles those who are unsure of their faith with the following message: "Let us examine our ways and test them, and let us return to the Lord." There are many ways for you to reopen your heart and mind to receiving God's love. Take some—or all—of the following steps and you will be on your way to accepting God back into your life, and your marriage.

- Read the Bible with your spouse.
- Attend church with your spouse once a week.
- Join a Bible study group for married couples.
- Give a copy of *How God Can Save Your Marriage in 40 Days* to your spouse as a gift.
- Participate in faith-based online chatrooms.
- Pray once a day.
- Visit with your pastor to discuss your doubts and marital fears.
- Find a congregation that suits your lifestyle and supports your values.
- Become active in church fundraisers and activities.

Will God Still Help Me If It's My Fault Our Marriage is Failing?

Yes! God helps those who help themselves. Your interest in saving your marriage has been clearly articulated with your investment in this book. Minor transgressions and outright sins do not have to equal a failed marriage. Confess your sins to Him, pray for forgiveness, and move forward with your life. Do not be stalled by past mistakes or all of the reasons you might fail. Rather, focus on completing every one of the exercises in this book and take the renewal of your relationship day by day. Trust that God loves you even with all of your sins and proceed toward redemption with your head held high. For as John 3:16 reminds us, "God so loved the world that He gave His one and only Son, that whoever believes in Him shall not perish, but have eternal life." Remember, God is on your side, and He wants your marriage to succeed.

Are There Certain Problems that Cannot Be Overcome?

Your mindset controls whether your problems as a couple strengthen or strangle your marriage. As Indian spiritual leader Mahatma Gandhi once said, "A man is but the product of his thoughts. What he thinks, he becomes." Decide that no mountain is too high to climb, and you will reach the summit. However, if you believe your troubles are insurmountable, then that will also become true. Let *How God Can Save Your Marriage in 40 Days* prove to you that colossal mistakes are no more difficult to overcome than minor irritations.

Take action right now, and don't pause to question whether your marital problems are too big to conquer. Think of what author Napoleon Hill once wrote: "Do not wait; the time will never be 'just right.' Start where you stand, and work with whatever tools you may have at your command, and better tools will be found as you go along." Don't slow the process of improving your marriage with doubt and hesitation. Jump into it with faith, love, and the belief that you can improve your relationship.

Indeed, do not spend another precious moment on fears that your attempt to save your marriage will fail—especially considering you haven't even yet tried. Your time is better spent putting the tips included in this book into action. There simply is no point in worrying about whether today's problems will still be here tomorrow. As Matthew 6:34 reminds us, "Do not worry about tomorrow, for tomorrow will worry about itself."

What If My Partner Wants a Divorce?

There are few things more painful in life than when a spouse declares he or she wants a divorce. Once the word "divorce" is thrown into the conversation, it is easy for all hope to be lost. The suggestion that the marriage ought to be dissolved means that one or both partners have given up on the relationship. People tend to give up on their marriages because of seemingly insurmountable problems like infidelity, irreconcilable differences or personality traits, or because they no longer feel in love. Indeed, when you face one or more of these problems, it can seem impossible to believe that your marriage can be saved.

But it can. The real problem with most marriages is that couples enter them with impossibly high expectations. Couples often imagine their lives will be a continuation of the fairytale that was their wedding. As a result, the true grit of domestic life shines a disappointing light on their relationship. One or both partners start to believe that the marriage is a letdown. When it is no longer shiny, new, romantic, and passionate, they think something is wrong. As a result, they stop working at the relationship and turn away from their marriage. Even at this point, though, a marriage can be saved.

Change your mind about what marriage means and you will have more than a fighting chance to save your relationship. Joseph Campbell, author of *The Power of Myth*, wisely observed, "When people get married because they think it's a long-time love affair, they'll be divorced very soon, because all love affairs end in disappointment. But marriage is a recognition of a spiritual identity." Through your commitment to the faithful execution of the exercises in this book, convince your partner that your connection is integral to both of your spiritual identities. Remind your spouse that your marriage is not the sum of its problems, but rather your combined effort at overcoming them.

Tools for Success

WHAT TO DO TO SAVE YOUR MARRIAGE

Keep a Journal

In addition to completing the exercises in this book, you are also asked to keep a written record of your progress, thoughts, fears, and observations over the course of the 40 days of this program. To this end, each of the 40 topics includes a reflection prompt that asks you to write about the particular day's topic. Space is given for you to write in this book itself, but if you need more room for your thoughts, consider keeping a separate journal. Regardless of which way you choose to write, do not skip this step, for it is an essential component of your self-exploration. Each of the writing assignments is designed to make you think about your actions, thoughts, and the way you treat and interact with your spouse. Each written exercise offers a private opportunity to admit difficult truths, work out personal demons, and vent frustrations without hurting your partner's feelings.

Be a faithful writer, and do not be limited by the reflection prompts. Write whatever you are moved to say, and use the prompts as a launching point to explore other ideas. Your journal is personal, but there may be times when you are asked to share a particular entry with your partner. Share your thoughts willingly, but keep your book close so it remains a safe space in which to share your most honest thoughts. Read aloud on the day you are called to share what you've written, but remind your spouse that your journal is otherwise private.

Choose a Trustworthy Person to Be Your Anchor

Select a trustworthy person to act as your sounding board, anchor, and cheerleader as you go through the next 40 days. Share with this person your goals for completing this program—to save your relationship from divorce, or to restore God's presence in your marriage, for example. Give your "40 days coach" a copy of *How God Can Save Your Marriage in 40 Days* so that he or she can follow your daily assignments. Turn to this person whenever you feel discouraged and ask them for the courage to continue. Likewise, share the positive results of your work so that your anchor person may cite examples of success when you need encouragement.

Have Faith in Your Relationship

The final tool at your disposal is faith that your relationship will live to see another day. Remind yourself that the current damaged state of your marriage is not necessarily relevant to its future success. As long as you can remember a time of love, kindness, passion, and friendship between you and your spouse, there is every reason to hope that your marriage will once again be the happy, fulfilling relationship that God meant it to be. With faith in your love and trust in God's good will, there is nothing you cannot accomplish. When it doubt, turn to Psalm 119:116 for encouragement. It asks of God, "Sustain me according to your promise, and I will live; do not let my hopes be dashed."

Your 40-Day Journey

TO

Save Your

MARRIAGE

Day 1

GOD WANTS YOU TO:
Recommit Yourself to Your Marriage

"The rain came down, the streams rose,
and the winds blew and beat against the house;
yet it did not fall, because it had its
foundation on the rock."

Matthew 7: 24-25

Do you remember your wedding vows?
When you entered into holy matrimony, you promised to love, honor, cherish, and obey your partner under God's watchful eyes. The vows you spoke at your wedding ceremony established your serious commitment to uphold the laws of marriage. Ecclesiastes 5:4 reminds us that God expects vows to be kept: "When you make a vow to God do not delay in fulfilling it. He has no pleasure in fools; fulfill your vow."

Relationships need maintenance
But over time, the drudgery of life can drain your energy to

the point where you stop making the effort to keep up your end of this holy contract. Many times, neither spouses notices that the rock upon which your marital foundation is built is breaking down until one day it splits from all the cracks. This can feel like a sudden, out-of-the-blue awakening. But in truth, relationship problems don't develop overnight—marriage requires regular maintenance to remain healthy and satisfying and stalls without constant care and upkeep.

Marriages can't be left on autopilot. When a couple stops practicing good communication skills, withholds affection, or forgets to be thankful for their spouse, each partner ends up feeling bored, neglected, or unloved. The signs of this are obvious, yet often ignored—spouses spend more time apart; they talk, laugh, hug, kiss, and have sex less often; and develop the mindset that it is up to the other person to fix the problem. However, marriage is a partnership between two people that cannot be fixed by just one of them.

Renew your vows in both word & deed
Rededicating yourself to your marriage will bring you a step closer toward rekindling the love and joy you felt for each other on your wedding day. Whether you send an email to your partner that says, "I do—again," or you make plans to have a formal vow renewal ceremony officiated by a minister, make your goal to be reminded of why you chose your partner in the first place. Then, choose each other all over again with every word and action you share.

YOUR DAILY | Act of Love

Mail a card to your partner. Your spouse will not expect mail from you, so it will be a sweet surprise! Write, "Thank you for marrying me. I wish every day was our wedding day!" Transcribe your vows on the card and add a new vow that you promise to keep from this day forward.

DATE ACCOMPLISHED: ....

DAILY REFLECTIONS: Write down examples of when you upheld or trespassed against your wedding vows. Then, draft a contract between you, your partner, and God that promises to faithfully execute all of the terms outlined in your vows.

....
....
....
....
....
....
....
....

ADDITIONAL WAYS
to improve your marriage

Too many couples try to force romance into their relationship when it's in trouble, believing that it signifies "true love." But as Friedrich Nietzsche warned, "It is not a lack of love, but a lack of friendship that makes unhappy marriages." Instead of focusing on the romantic element in your marriage, nurture the friendship you have developed with your spouse. Think of friendship as the rock on which your marriage is built. Play, laugh, talk, and do things together as you would with your best friend. Let romance blossom naturally out of your rediscovered affection for spending time together as friends.

3 exercises to help you incorporate today's theme

❶ Keep a box of thank you cards in your desk at work. Send one to your spouse whenever you want to express your appreciation in a special way.

❷ Write one new wedding vow per month and share them all with your partner on your anniversary.

❸ List 5 reasons you are glad you married your partner, and share them with your spouse:

① ....

② ....

③ ....

④ ....

⑤ ....

Day 2

GOD WANTS YOU TO:
Pray Together to Stay Together

"So what shall I do? I will pray with my spirit, but
I will also pray with my mind; I will sing with my
spirit, but I will also sing with my mind."

1 Corinthians 14:15

**The connection you have with God affects the quality of
your marriage**

When you and your partner pray together, you reestablish
the three-way relationship you, your spouse, and God
entered into on your wedding day. Praying with your partner
serves as a daily reminder that your marriage was ordained
by God—that the connection you have with Him directly
influences the connection you have with your spouse. Praying
together plugs both of you into His divine presence. It also
creates a space and time to be thankful and to seek guidance
during troubled times. As Matthew 18:20 reminds us, "For
where two or three come together in my name, there am I
with them."

View prayer as an opportunity

Use prayer as an opportunity to express gratitude to God

for the people and things in your life. Couples who do so are happier with the present and more optimistic about the future.

Couples who pray together have a more positive outlook because:

• Shared invocations encourage people to work together to do a better job of living up to God's Word.
• The Spiritual Science Research Foundation notes that prayer improves "action, thought, and attitude," all of which have a significant impact on a marriage's success.

Reaping the benefits of prayer is simple. Schedule a few minutes with your partner to discuss what you are thankful for that day, and then send a joint message to God.

Let truth guide your prayers
Praying together also provides an opportunity to confess sins and to ask for forgiveness. As James 5:16 advises, "Confess your sins to each other and pray for each other so that you may be healed. The prayer of a righteous man is powerful and effective." Use prayer as a way to right wrongs with your spouse in the presence of God. Confess mistakes both large and small, and vow not to repeat them. However, do not exaggerate good intentions or downplay the extent of your transgressions. For as Leviticus 19:12 warns, "You must not make a false promise by my name, or you will show that you don't respect your God." Let truth be your guide when asking for forgiveness. When given to God with pure intentions, prayer has the ability to restore peace, lift spirits, offer absolution, and make instantaneous changes.

YOUR DAILY | Act of Love

Choose a quiet time of day to pray with your partner, such as first thing in the morning or just before bed. Hold your partner's hands, face each other, and say, "Let's thank God together for all of our blessings." With your hands clasped, take turns saying things for which you each feel blessed. Feel the exchange of loving energy between you, your partner, and God.

DATE ACCOMPLISHED: ....

DAILY REFLECTIONS: The next time you pray together, reflect on how prayer connects you, your partner, and God in a sort of triangle where each side strengthens the others. Writing about this intimate relationship should remind you of the lifelong connection you made on your wedding day.

....
....
....
....
....
....
....
....

ADDITIONAL WAYS
to improve your marriage

Pray together to express to each other—and to God—that you and your spouse have mutual interests, ideas, and concerns. Use it as a time to exhibit unity and fellowship in your shared love for God and his Word. Think of praying with your partner like constructing a building. This shelter protects your marriage from threatening influences. View it as a means for strengthening your spiritual bonds with God, which reinforces your marriage at its very foundation. Take all of your problems to God as a team, because praying together makes it tough to remain confused, afraid, or angry with each other.

3 exercises to help you incorporate today's theme

❶ Buy a box of prayer cards and give half to your partner. Each day, take turns selecting and reciting a prayer from your stack of cards. Exchange the cards after each invocation and discuss how the prayer applies to your marriage.

❷ Print your favorite prayer on high-quality paper. Then frame it and give it to your partner as a present. Write a note explaining why it is meaningful to you.

❸ If you have children, include them in family prayer at mealtime and before bed.

Day 3

GOD WANTS YOU TO:
Get Closer Through Bible Study

"Let the word of Christ dwell in you richly as you teach and admonish one another with all wisdom, and as you sing psalms, hymns and spiritual songs with gratitude in your hearts to God."

Colossians 3:16-17

Using the Bible to communicate with each other

Couples who read and discuss the Bible together are more likely to enjoy a stimulating exchange of ideas about religion and other important topics. Bible study encourages couples to explore each other's points of view not only on scripture but also on politics, relationships, values, and more. It also highlights God's presence in and around those who follow his teachings. For as it reads in 1 John 2:5, "If anyone obeys his word, God's love is truly made complete in him. This is how we know we are in him."

Use the Bible as a tool

When trouble strikes, use the Bible as a troubleshooting guide to your relationship. You will be astonished by how often the Bible provides a solution to your problem. With so many practical pieces of advice and lovely insights into human nature, it is no wonder the Bible is the world's most widely read book. Use your Bible study sessions to identify these pieces of wisdom with your partner.

- Consult the books Proverbs and Gospels for practical guidelines on how to live up to God's expectations.
- Study 1 Corinthians 13:4-7 with your partner to be reminded of God's definition of love.
- Find a solution in the Bible to a problem, and share it with your partner.
- Allow your relationship with your partner to mature through careful study and application of scripture.

Use the Bible as a tool to enrich your relationship with God— and with each other. Over time you will notice an enhanced connection with your spouse as your understanding of God's word deepens.

Live the Word

To get the most out of Bible study, both you and your partner must live according to the Word. After all, there is no point in reading and discussing passages when one of you acts contrary to Christ's teachings. Taking action, therefore, is critical to turning what is discussed during Bible study into a reality for your relationship. Practice what you learn by using the last 15 minutes of each study session to discuss ways you and your partner can implement the lessons of the passages you've talked about.

YOUR DAILY | Act of Love

Turn Bible study into a regular date night! Attend
weekly, early-evening classes and follow them up with
dinner out. Over your meal, discuss insights, thoughts,
and help each other gain a deeper understanding of the
lesson. Prepare for the next week's study by reading
passages aloud and discussing their meaning. Take turns
choosing a restaurant each week to keep the date
night component alive.

DATE ACCOMPLISHED: ....

DAILY REFLECTIONS: Think of the Bible as a guide book for
how to maximize the quality and longevity of your marriage.
Write down problems you face as a couple as well as solutions
to them found in the Bible.

....

....

....

....

....

....

....

....

ADDITIONAL WAYS
to improve your marriage

Matthew 4:4 reads, "Man does not live on bread alone, but on every word that comes from the mouth of God." Consider Bible study with your partner as essential nourishment for your marriage. Savor each morsel of God's wisdom as food for thought, and never deprive your relationship of nutritious Holy Scripture. To drive home the point that God's Word is food for your relationship, literally break bread with your partner during Bible study. During flavorful meals, acknowledge that you are privileged to share each blessed bite with your spouse.

3 exercises to help you incorporate today's theme

❶ Suggest that your married friends take turns hosting a weekly Bible study at their homes. Offer to host the first one, and make it a potluck.

❷ Surprise your partner with a new Bible inscribed with a special message.

❸ Start a Bible blog where you, your partner, and your family and friends can share thoughts about scripture and how it relates to the day's events.

Day 4

GOD WANTS YOU TO:
Listen with an Open Heart

"Everyone should be quick to listen, slow
to speak and slow to become angry."

James 1:19

Multitasking inhibits your ability to listen

Americans are not talking face-to-face as often as they used
to. Their active listening skills have been rendered somewhat
archaic by impersonal methods of communication like email,
online chat, text messages, and social media. In addition,
many couples are overscheduled and forced to multi-task.
For example, they might be reduced to discussing their
child's performance in school while on their cell phones
running different household errands. Likewise, discussions
about finances happen while sending emails, surfing the web,
or loading the dishwasher; chats about family vacations or
events are worked into the 20 minutes before one leaves for
work. Overall, couples are distracted and thus unable to
listen to each other as well as they should.

When people multitask while listening, they miss out on

important information and emotional cues. They are more likely to misinterpret their partner's meaning or blank on important dates and commitments. When you divide your attention your brain cannot fully commit to any one task. Consequently, arguments blow up out of misunderstandings that result from half-hearted attempts to listen.

Reduce distractions to become a better listener
Becoming a skilled listener requires dedication and discipline. The first step is to limit distractions. During conversations with your spouse:

- Turn off the television.
- Step away from the computer.
- Turn off the ringer on your cell phone.
- Leave PDAs in your briefcase/purse.
- Talk in a room with minimal noise and potential for interruptions.

Once distractions have been removed, you can focus 100 percent of your attention on communicating with your partner. This lets you truly hear your partner's views, concerns, and expectations. Giving your undivided attention to your partner fulfills an often unmet need to feel listened to and acknowledged. Deuteronomy 5:27 offers the following reminder on the importance of listening: "Go near and listen to all that the Lord our God says. Then tell us whatever the Lord our God tells you. We will listen and obey."

YOUR DAILY | Act of Love

Make listening a regular part of your routine. In the morning ask your partner, "What do you have planned for today?" In the afternoon call to say, "I just wanted to hear how your day is going." In the evening inquire about an issue you know is important to your partner. In each instance, listen to your spouse with your entire body. Do nothing else—don't do dishes, send emails—just listen.

DATE ACCOMPLISHED: ....

DAILY REFLECTIONS: Jot down thoughts about how crossed arms, a turned back, or lack of eye contact might be interpreted by your partner. Use what you come up with as a tool to remind you to pay attention to your own body language when your partner talks to you.

....

....

....

....

....

....

....

....

DAY

4

ADDITIONAL WAYS
to improve your marriage

It's hard to take into account your partner's concerns and frustrations when you get defensive upon hearing them. When you jump to explanations, retorts, and arguments, your partner's message gets lost. Step outside of yourself and focus on your partner's concerns. Acknowledge where they are valid. Give him or her space to air any grievances. Let your spouse know you see where he or she is coming from. Regardless of how badly you want to defend yourself, follow the advice of 1 Kings 8:52, which reads, "May your eyes be open to your servant's plea and to the plea of your people Israel, and may you listen to them whenever they cry out to you."

3 exercises to help you incorporate today's theme

❶ Use reflective listening by repeating back what you think your partner said. For example, "What I hear you saying is that you are frustrated that your boss doesn't reward hard work."

❷ Make eye contact with your partner during conversations and arguments—even when it's difficult.

❸ Listen to your partner without planning what to say next.

Day 5

GOD WANTS YOU TO:
Be Willing to Forgive

"Clothe yourselves with compassion, kindness,
humility, gentleness and patience. Bear with each
other and forgive whatever grievances you may have
against one another. Forgive as the
Lord forgave you."

Colossians 3:12-13

Give your partner the gift of forgiveness
Forgiveness is a powerful gift. It costs nothing, yet bestows priceless rewards on both the giver and the receiver. Indeed, the simple act of saying, "I'm sorry" soothes even the deepest wounds with peace and comfort. Give absolution freely to your partner—it prevents bitterness and resentment from damaging your relationship. Hanging onto anger, jealousy, and injustice causes hurt to fester. Before long, it turns into a painful knot that threatens to choke the life out of your marriage. Use forgiveness as a way to untie the noose created by such grudges.

Be the first to say "I'm sorry."

Issuing a pardon to your spouse allows each of you to be moved. You move past the experience of being wronged; your spouse moves out of the doghouse and back into your good graces. Forgiveness also restores the balance of power in your relationship, allowing it to move into a deeper, more mature place. Saying "I'm sorry" demonstrates your strong commitment to love over the need to be right. Your partner is likely to be moved by your humility and follow suit. Once you have taken steps toward forgiving each other, true communication can begin.

Forgive so that you may be forgiven

You have undoubtedly made mistakes or committed sins that require God's forgiveness in addition to your partner's. But the Bible states that you must forgive others before being forgiven. Mark 11:25 reminds us: "And when you stand praying, if you hold anything against anyone, forgive him, so that your Father in heaven may forgive you your sins." Pray for God's help to forgive serious infractions made by your spouse, and feel the cycle of forgiveness take root.

YOUR DAILY | Act of Love

Forgive your spouse today for any transgressions, big or small. Make it known that as far as you are concerned, today begins a clean slate. Release old grudges and avoid developing new ones. As an act of symbolism, write down your resentments and then burn or shred them. Once destroyed, vow never to resurrect the issues laid to rest with that list.

DATE ACCOMPLISHED: ....

DAILY REFLECTIONS: Write about why you are unable to let a particular issue go. Use your written thoughts to explore whether you hold on to it because you are truly wounded or because you have a need to punish your partner.

....

....

....

....

....

....

....

....

ADDITIONAL WAYS
to improve your marriage

Holding on to a grudge can rot your interactions with your spouse. Instead of draining the love from your marriage, make efforts to inject happiness and calm into your relationship. Switch from blaming your partner to enjoying him or her the way you did before "the incident." Some tips for easing your way into forgiving your partner include:

- Never withhold affection from your spouse.
- Take note of efforts your partner has made to change, and comment on them.
- Privately chant the phrase, "I forgive you," during quiet meditation.
- Laugh heartily when your spouse says something funny.

3 exercises to help you incorporate today's theme

❶ Make a list of grievances you hold against your partner. One last time, consider the details of each one—then cross them off your list. After doing so, avoid thinking of them ever again.

❷ Ask your partner to forgive you for any wrongdoings or pain you have caused. Give a heartfelt apology, and do not expect your partner to offer immediate forgiveness.

❸ Ask God for the strength to forgive your partner.

Day 6

GOD WANTS YOU TO:
Love Being Vulnerable

"And we rejoice in the hope of the glory of God.
Not only so, but we also rejoice in our sufferings,
because we know that suffering produces perseverance; perseverance, character; and character, hope."

Romans 5:2-4

Let your guard down

It can be scary to strip away your defenses in front of your
partner, because in the process you remove your protective
layers. Making oneself vulnerable can feel a bit like standing
naked in front of a firing squad. But to become one with
your spouse (as you promised to do in your wedding vows),
you must drop your guard and let your partner in—all the
way in. Remember, you chose your partner and thus should
trust that he or she will take gentle care of you in your most
exposed moments.

Vulnerability means being honest

God expects us to be honest with Him, with each other,
and to operate with integrity in our relationships. This is

why it is written in 1 Chronicles 29:17, "I know, my God, that you test the heart and are pleased with integrity. All these things have I given willingly and with honest intent. And now I have seen with joy how willingly your people who are here have given to you." Try opening your heart and mind to your partner in ways that feel new—and even a little scary—to you. It may be more than you are used to giving, but you owe it to your partner to share fears, private feelings, and untested ideas. Some suggestions for how to practice being vulnerable include:

- Express the magnitude of your feelings.
  For example: "I love you so much, sometimes it just stops me in my tracks."
- Share the details of a pipe dream with your spouse.
  Allow yourself to be excited as you relay your ideal scenario for making it happen.
- Openly discuss fears about aging, illness, and death.
- Circulate a piece of writing you are passionate about to your friends, or hang something you painted in your home. Hearing people's comments on work you might be unsure about is good practice for becoming vulnerable to criticism.

Choose connection over ego

When you avoid risk to protect your ego, you miss out on making true connections with your spouse. As Helen Keller once wrote, "Avoiding danger is no safer in the long run than outright exposure. Life is either a daring adventure or nothing." Indeed, it is in the most vulnerable moments with each other that couples indulge their greatest passions and experience their most exciting adventures.

YOUR DAILY | Act of Love

Many couples avoid feeling vulnerable by hiding thoughts, feelings, and information from each other. But to be close is to be vulnerable, so embrace this most intimate connection with your partner. Get closer to your partner by revealing a secret fear to him or her today. This can range from "I am afraid of being replaced by younger workers at my job," to "I worry you won't be attracted to me when I am X years old."

DATE ACCOMPLISHED: ....

DAILY REFLECTIONS: Make a list of what you fear most about becoming vulnerable to your partner. How realistic is it that this fear will be realized? And what are the benefits of taking the risk anyway?

....
....
....
....
....
....
....
....

ADDITIONAL WAYS

to improve your marriage

Being vulnerable with your spouse doesn't mean giving up your right to privacy. Use the following tips for getting close to your partner while retaining personal boundaries:

- Share excerpts of your journal that showcase your feelings about significant events, fights, or experiences with your partner. Meanwhile, keep your diary personal and private from your spouse.

- Trust your partner with a list of passwords to your various online accounts, including email, Facebook, and online banking sites. Trust that your spouse will not access your accounts unless you ask him or her to or there is an emergency.

3 exercises to help you incorporate today's theme

❶ Strip down and get in bed naked with your partner. Have a difficult conversation covered only by a sheet and really allow yourself to feel vulnerable. Trust your partner will make you feel safe enough to express yourself in this state.

❷ The next time you cry, do it in front of your partner.

❸ Write a letter to your spouse that expresses your love, commitment, excitements and fears about marriage.

Day 7

GOD WANTS YOU TO:
Let Your Finances
Be an Open Book

"Keep your lives free from the love of money
and be content with what you have."

Hebrews 13:5

Be honest about your financial habits

A 2004 *Smart Money/Redbook* survey found that although
70 percent of couples discussed money matters at least once
a week, most ended up in arguments anyway. One reason
couples fight even when they communicate regularly about
finances is because 36 percent of men and 40 percent of
women lie about how much they actually spend. Make
money talks work for your relationship by providing a
complete financial picture for your spouse. Don't hide any
fact about your spending: confess to all lattés, shoes, CDs,
and happy-hour cocktails purchased throughout the week.

Share all sources of income with your spouse

All money earned should be disclosed to your partner—even minor winnings or dividends from investments purchased before you were married. Examples of income sources to add to financial discussions include:

- Annual salary increases, merit raises, and bonuses
- Lottery and contest winnings
- Money won through gambling and office pools
- Alimony or child support from a previous marriage
- Settlements from lawsuits
- Money earned from the sale of personal property
- Interest-earning accounts, such as savings and CDs

In addition to sharing the existence of such monies with your partner, share the reality of them too. Avoid thinking that because certain dividends were earned from your investments that the money is solely yours to spend.

Come clean about personal debt

Dishonesty about personal debt ranked as the number one reason couples argued, according to the *Smart Money/ Redbook* survey. Schedule a time to discuss how you can work together to attack your debt as a team. In the spirit of full disclosure, produce financial statements and print a free copy of your credit report for your partner to see.

Stick to spending limits

Agree to spending limits with your partner and then stick to them. If you feel the urge to splurge beyond the agreed upon allowance, check in with your partner and have a discussion about the item in question.

YOUR DAILY | Act of Love

Choose today to open a joint checking account with your partner. Each pay period, agree to contribute a certain amount of money to the account to cover bills and entertainment enjoyed together. Even if just one person handles the household finances, the other will feel included. Both partners will also be able to track joint purchases online.

DATE ACCOMPLISHED: ....

DAILY REFLECTIONS: List any financial secrets you keep from your spouse. Do you ever hide, lie about, or downplay personal expenses, such as meals out, drinks with friends, or online purchases? If so, why do you think you do it?

....
....
....
....
....
....
....
....

ADDITIONAL WAYS
to improve your marriage

Avoid statements such as, "I can't believe you wasted $100 on a new dress!" When your partner hears the word "wasted" she feels as though you are passing judgment on her taste and the way she chooses to spend money. She is likely to become defensive, and you will end up in an argument. One suggestion for eliminating these kinds of fights is to agree to a No Questions Asked fund. In other words, decide that you each get to spend a certain amount per week on whatever you want, without explanation. Use this money as a freedom allowance and feel free to spend it on food, fun, clothes, books, gadgets, sports equipment, and novelty items that are just for you.

3 exercises to help you incorporate today's theme

❶ For one month, collect receipts for all purchases, big and small. Sit down with your spouse at the end of each month to add up expenses. Share ideas for cutting costs over the next 30 days.

❷ Set up online banking profiles with your partner so that you can each track your accounts remotely.

❸ Join an investment club for couples who have similar goals, such as saving for kids' tuition, retirement, or buying a first home.

Day 8

GOD WANTS YOU TO:
Be Your Partner's Number One Fan

"I will praise you, O Lord, with all my heart; I will tell of all your wonders. I will be glad and rejoice in you; I will sing praise to your name, O Most High."

Psalm 9:1-2

Be generous with your praise
Promote good feelings in your marriage by frequently praising your partner. Acknowledge every accomplishment with a sincere compliment. Praise-worthy actions include when your partner completes a home-improvement project, earns a promotion, reaches a milestone, or sticks to an exercise routine. Note also when your spouse takes on extra responsibilities at work or around the house, and tell him or her that you appreciate the extra effort. Be generous with your praise, and offer it not just in private but when you are both around friends and family.

DAY 8

Remember that when you praise your partner, you also praise God's creation. 1 Chronicles 16:9 advises, "Sing to him, sing praise to him; tell of all his wonderful acts." With this in mind, know that God is pleased when you revel in your partner's accomplishments as if they were your own.

Criticize sparingly

Visualize your spouse as a balloon that is kept afloat by love, kindness, and compassion. Imagine that each nice thing you say to your partner gives the balloon a little blast of helium that makes it fly a bit higher. Now imagine that each critical word you speak lets air out of the balloon, causing it to sink. It is your duty in marriage to lift your partner up, just as God's love promises to hold up his followers: "If I rise on the wings of the dawn, if I settle on the far side of the sea, even there your hand will guide me." (Psalm 139:9-10)

Leave mistakes in the past

Truly celebrate the person your partner is at this moment and leave his or her mistakes in the past. Isaiah 43:18 tells us to "forget the former things; do not dwell on the past." Yet it is difficult for most people to let bygones be. Instead of constantly resurrecting old hurts, put a positive spin on such moments. View them as stepping stones to the people you are at this point in time, or as tests that bonded you to each other even more fiercely. Cheer how far your relationship has come. Remember, all couples endure trials and struggles, but it is how they react to such struggles that makes or breaks them as a couple. In your relationship, vow to celebrate progress. Then, never look back as you mature both as individuals and as a couple.

YOUR DAILY | Act of Love

Tell everyone you talk to today that you are proud of your partner. Allow admiration to fill your heart as you pick one specific quality or accomplishment to highlight. For example, let your spouse overhear a telephone conversation in which you sing his or her praises. Boast to friends that he or she earned a promotion, has stellar parenting skills, or cooked a delicious meal.

DATE ACCOMPLISHED: ....

DAILY REFLECTIONS: Write down the last time you remember congratulating your spouse on an achievement. Assess whether you tend to complain about your partner more often than you praise him or her, and explore why.

....
....
....
....
....
....
....
....

ADDITIONAL WAYS

to improve your marriage

Charles Dickens once wrote, "Fan the sinking flame of hilarity with the wing of friendship; and pass the rosy wine." In his whimsical style, Dickens was trying to say that sometimes the best thing you can do for your relationship is not to take it so seriously. Take a hiatus from arguments and somber discussions and treat your partner as your best friend. Share a bottle of wine and laugh heartily together. Start a jovial conversation about what you like best about him and finish the following sentence: "I am in love with you because _____." Turn this exercise into a lighthearted game, and make the goal to improve your partner's mood and overall outlook.

3 exercises to help you incorporate today's theme

❶ Send your partner an email or text message that says, "I can't get over what a great job you did on the garage" or "I am still smiling thinking of that delicious meal you made last night." Or, keep it simple and just write, "You rock!"

❷ Make your compliments informed by actually looking over the work your partner produces. Read reports he writes or plans she designs. This way, when you tell your partner "great job," you will really know what you are talking about. Additionally, it will show you are taking an active interest in his or her work.

❸ Email, call, or mail announcements to friends and family to alert them to your partner's latest accomplishment. This could be a recognition or promotion she earned at work, a piece of art or writing he produced, or an athletic achievement reached.

Day 9

GOD WANTS YOU TO:

Give Thanks for Your Partner

"Give thanks in all circumstances, for this is
God's will for you in Christ Jesus."

1 Thessalonians 5:18

Think of your partner as a gift from God

When you live together, it is easy forget that your spouse is
more than just another body living in your home; that he or
she is, in fact, a special gift from God. As such, He expects
you to give thanks for every moment you get to share with
your spouse—from morning breath to snoring slumber.

Of course, it is not realistic to thank God every minute
of the day, but most people neglect to give thanks at all.
Therefore, aim to express gratitude at least once a day. Take
the opportunity to reflect on how your partner adds to your
quality of life. Be grateful to God for leading you to the
most significant person in your life. It may even help to flash
forward to later in your lives, to a time when each of you
might be less healthy and happy than you are today. Think

of how vulnerable, scared, and lonely you will be when that time comes, and use those emotions to feel grateful for every minute you get to spend together at this moment in time.

Show your appreciation for your spouse

The great Roman philosopher Cicero wisely wrote, "Gratitude is not only the greatest of virtues, but the parent of all the others." Demonstrate the greatest of virtues and let God know how much you appreciate that He granted love, companionship, and friendship to your marriage. Let every word and deed represent little thank you cards to both God and your spouse. Engage in the following acts of appreciation:

- Surprise your spouse at work with lunch from his favorite restaurant.
- Clean the house before your partner gets home from work. Leave a note on the refrigerator that reads, "You deserve to come home to a clean house!"
- Send flowers to your partner at work with a card that reads, "I am lucky to have you as my wife!"
- Send an email to your spouse with a list of 5 reasons you are thankful to be married to him. Write "You are God's gift to me!" in the subject line.
- Remember to thank God for your partner in your daily devotionals.

YOUR DAILY | Act of Love

Today, use special stationery to write a prayer thanking God for your partner, and make a copy for yourself. Give the original to your spouse and recite it throughout the day. Include in your prayer concrete examples of thoughtful acts, admirable attributes, and specific reasons why you cherish your partner. Above all, do this without expecting to be praised in return.

DATE ACCOMPLISHED: ....

DAILY REFLECTIONS: Write down ways you can express gratitude for the work your spouse does—on the job, at home, in personal endeavors, and with your children. List ways you can you regularly communicate to your partner that you appreciate him or her.

....

....

....

....

....

....

....

....

DAY
9

ADDITIONAL WAYS
to improve your marriage

Too many of us get bogged down being irritated by small things about our partners. But when you make an effort to focus on your spouse's greatest attributes, it is easy to let minor annoyances go. Create a comprehensive list of what you like best about your partner. These can be physical attributes, personality traits, or even ways and manners your partner has. Refer to this list whenever you need a reminder for why you married your spouse in the first place. Go a step further and share your "What I Love About You" list with your partner. Above all, use this list as a constant reminder to treat your partner with love and respect. For as President John F. Kennedy, Jr. once said, "As we express our gratitude, we must never forget that the highest appreciation is not to utter words, but to live by them."

3 exercises to help you incorporate today's theme

❶ Make a small donation to your church and ask the minister or priest to make special mention of your spouse at the next service. Or, make a donation to an organization you know your partner respects. Doing so will help her know that you enjoy honoring him or her not just with your words, but with your actions.

❷ Sing your favorite hymn and dedicate it to your partner.

❸ Write a love letter to your spouse, and wait for the perfect moment to surprise him or her with it.

56 • How God Can Save Your Marriage in 40 Days

Day 10

GOD WANTS YOU TO:

Rest Together, Play Together

"The seventh day is a Sabbath to the Lord your
God. On it you shall not do any work."

Exodus 20:10

Have fun together

Self-improvement writer Dale Carnegie once said, "People
rarely succeed unless they have fun in what they are doing."
Carnegie was right—think of how awful it is to do a chore
you particularly hate. It seems to drag on forever, you resent
doing it, and so you exert minimal effort to get it done.
Such lackluster attempts to accomplish a goal usually yield
unimpressive results. On the other hand, when you enjoy
what you do, success comes fast and easy. The same is true
about working at and saving your marriage. Therefore, if
you do not have fun doing the work needed to repair your
relationship, your chances of success are not very high.

Unfortunately, many couples—especially struggling ones—
have forgotten how to have fun together. They get caught
up in the business end of running a household and forget
to be silly and playful. Lack of lighthearted companionship
inevitably leads to general dissatisfaction and arguments.

Eventually, your relationship is ruled by tension instead of camaraderie. It is natural to wonder whether you have anything left in common when you reach this point.

You must overcome this joyless state and resurrect your relationship's spirit of fun. When you do it will remind you of all the goodness you and your partner share. Try out the following fun suggestions in your relationship:

- Go to the gym together.
- Cook a nice meal together, and grocery shop for the ingredients together, too.
- Challenge your partner to a board game.
- Surprise your spouse with tickets to a play.
- Plan a vacation or weekend getaway and make figuring out the details together part of the fun.

Schedule quiet time with your spouse
Most couples are overworked, overscheduled, and have little time to relax together. But quiet time is critical for recharging and reconnecting. And when you make time for it, it demonstrates that your relationship is your top priority. Overcome any scheduling issues by booking downtime with your partner. Set aside one day a week to do next to nothing together. Suggestions for sharing low-key time include:

- Share a pot of tea or a bottle of wine.
- Do a crossword puzzle together.
- Buy two copies of a book, read it at the same time, and discuss your thoughts on it over dinner.
- Give each other shoulder massages.
- Listen to music and lounge together on the couch.

YOUR DAILY | Act of Love

Dedicate one day a week to leisure and rest to bring out the playful, loving side of your relationship. Plan a full day to revive your best friendship by doing something fun together. See a movie, go bowling, or toss a Frisbee in the park. Later, lie in bed and discuss anything that comes to mind—as long as it has nothing to do with your domestic responsibilities or financial hardships.

DATE ACCOMPLISHED: ....

DAILY REFLECTIONS: Write down how the leisure time you share with your spouse has changed since you got married. As you write, think about when it was that you last went on a walk with your partner, or played a game instead of watching TV. What can you do to make more time to be together?

....
....
....
....
....
....
....
....

ADDITIONAL WAYS
to improve your marriage

German philosopher Arthur Schopenhauer once wrote, "The two foes of human happiness are pain and boredom." With this in mind, shake up the monotony of your routine by doing something thrilling with your partner. Adventurous couples might try skydiving or taking scuba diving or rock climbing lessons together. For those looking for a lower-octane thrill, train for a physical challenge together, such as a marathon or bike trip. Regular physical activity improves mental and physical health. It also has a positive impact on your overall mood because exercise releases endorphins—natural pain relievers that make you feel happy and bonded.

3 exercises to help you incorporate today's theme

❶ Establish a sleep schedule that involves your partner. Take a nap with your partner on weekends, linger in bed together in the mornings, and try to go to bed at the same time.

❷ Plan a family day at the park or the beach. Pack a picnic lunch, a blanket, and a Frisbee, volleyball, or Whiffle Ball set.

❸ Play road trip games in the car, such as "I spy" or "Name that Tune." Or, keep a deck of Trivial Pursuit cards in the glove compartment and quiz whoever is driving. Finally, purchase or borrow books on tape or comedy routines. These fill long car trips with laughs and lightness.

Day 11

GOD WANTS YOU TO:

Express Love through Touch

"The wife's body does not belong to her alone
but also to her husband. In the same way, the
husband's body does not belong to him
alone but also to his wife."

1 Corinthians 7:4

Be affectionate in public

In high school, public displays of affection (PDA) were off-limits. Because PDA was so frowned upon, it was exciting to sneak smooches between classes or hold hands under the lunch table. Though the days of having to hide your love are long past, you can still generate the passion that is ignited by PDA. Spontaneous kisses and surprise embraces will light your partner's fire. So practice giving them while at the grocery store, at a party, or when walking down the street. It will make both you and your partner feel special and young again.

Make time to cuddle

Cuddling has many benefits. It fosters intimacy and physical connection and has been shown to release the bonding hormone oxytocin. Set your alarm 15 minutes early a few mornings a week. Use this time to lie in bed and hold your spouse. Nuzzle her neck, lay your head on his chest, and ground your day in the physical connection you have with your partner.

Become one with your partner through sex

Ephesians 5:31 declares, "A man will leave his father and mother and be united to his wife, and the two will become one flesh." Sex is the most literal way in which a husband and wife can become one flesh. Indeed, foreplay and sexual intercourse are the ultimate means for expressing your love for your partner's mind, body, and spirit.

Use sexual intimacy as an alternate language for conveying your passion and adoration for your spouse. Deliver every stroke, motion, and sound lovingly and with genuine affection. Don't use this time to think about your grocery list or the pile of work waiting on your desk. In other words, always be 100 percent in the moment and savor every touch, taste, and scent during your lovemaking experience. Finally, be willing to experiment with the following in the bedroom:

- Try a new position.
- Bring your partner to orgasm without expecting one in return.
- Describe out loud how good it feels as your partner gives you pleasure.

YOUR DAILY | Act of Love

Today, start touching your partner whenever you are in the same room. Small gestures will convey big feelings. Put your hand on the small of her back. Hold his hand for a moment before dinner. Hug and kiss your spouse hello, goodbye, good morning, and goodnight. Hold each other for at least a minute before parting company, getting out of bed, or falling asleep.

DATE ACCOMPLISHED: ....

DAILY REFLECTIONS: Keep a record of how often you convey physical affection for your partner. Use it as a reminder to touch your spouse at least 3 times a day to maintain physical intimacy.

....

....

....

....

....

....

....

....

ADDITIONAL WAYS
to improve your marriage

Never withhold affection or sex from your partner as punishment for a wrongdoing or after you've had an argument. Such behavior is passive-aggressive and will breed hostility in your marriage. Besides, the longer you withhold affection, the more difficult it is to resume your normal, intimate relationship.

If something is bothering you, talk about it with your partner. After the discussion or argument, be the first one to hug or kiss your spouse, even if you don't feel like doing so. In many cases, initiating physical intimacy immediately after a fight can heal hurt feelings and wounded egos faster than an apology does.

3 exercises to help you incorporate today's theme

❶ Enroll in a massage class with your partner. Practice the techniques you learn in class often.

❷ Give your spouse a bear-hug from behind.

❸ Always kiss your partner goodnight, and especially after you've had a disagreement. You will sleep better, and there is a good chance that the argument will be over when you wake up in the morning.

Day 12

GOD WANTS YOU TO:
Put Your Partner's Needs Ahead of Your Own

"Do nothing out of selfish ambition or vain conceit, but in humility consider others better than yourselves. Each of you should look not only to your own interests, but also to the interests of others."
Philippians 2:3-4

Serve God by helping your partner
In 2 Kings 4:2, Elisha asks the widow, "How can I help you?" When the widow explains she cannot afford to pay her creditors, a miracle occurs. Elisha advises the widow to pour oil from her one full container into empty jars borrowed from neighbors. The oil flows freely, and she is able to fill up all of the borrowed jars to sell and pay off her creditors. The moral of the story is that Elisha had faith that the Lord would work miracles through her if she served others.

Like Elisha, trust that when you help your partner, God is working through you. Let Him guide you to perform deeds

that improve your partner's quality of life. Remember that even small efforts to ease your partner's burdens can feel like little miracles when they relieve stress and brighten his or her day. Perform the following simple acts of kindness:

- Offer to carry groceries in from the car.
- Fill up the gas tank in your partner's car.
- Pick up your spouse's dry cleaning on your way home.
- Let your partner rest while you clean the house.
- Get take-out whenever your spouse works late.
- Say "yes" to your partner's seductions more often than you say "no."
- Give the dog a bath.
- Put freshly laundered sheets on the bed.
- Divvy up special occasion and holiday party planning duties.

Lead by example

You can lead the way toward a more caring marriage when you take time to notice what dissatisfies or annoys your spouse. Inquire about the problem, and then work together to find a solution, even if it means temporarily sacrificing your own needs. Some examples include working a little overtime to finance her Pilates classes or relieving him of childcare duties on the weekend so he can play golf with his friends. Consistently put your partner's needs ahead of your own to demonstrate that he or she is your top priority. Over time, your selfless acts will add up and raise the bar for how you treat each other. Your partner will eventually catch on and behave in the same way, greatly improving your marriage.

YOUR DAILY | Act of Love

Today, make it a point to do one selfless act. Your goal is to relieve your partner of at least one burden. Ask your husband what you can do to make his day better, and then do it. Or, better yet, intuit what needs to be done and do it without asking. For example, take the trash out and tell your wife you'll be picking up the kids after school. Don't expect to be thanked or compensated. Rather, let lightening your partner's load be its own reward.

DATE ACCOMPLISHED: ....

DAILY REFLECTIONS: Jot down examples of how you put your partner's needs ahead of your own. Use the following questions as writing prompts: Do you tend to act in your own best interest? How can you make your spouse feel like more of a priority? What could your partner do to make you feel like your needs are important?

....

....

....

....

....

....

....

....

DAY
__
12

ADDITIONAL WAYS
to improve your marriage

Never let your partner feel as though his or her basic needs are continually and chronically left unmet. People who feel as though their lives are bankrupt of affection, connection, sex, joy, and a healthy lifestyle are deeply unhappy. Consequently, their marriages suffer, because they are consumed with thoughts about what they lack rather than what they have.

With this in mind, give generously of your time, body, spirituality, and good humor. Frequently check in with your partner to find out whether he or she feels any of his or her fundamental needs have gone unmet. Come up with a plan to improve his or her quality of life—as well as the state of your relationship.

3 exercises to help you incorporate today's theme

❶ For one month, take over a chore that normally falls onto your partner's plate. For example, make the children's lunches, put yourself in charge of doing the laundry, or take over mowing the lawn.

❷ One day this week, leave the following note for your spouse, "List 5 things I can do to make life easier for you this week. Love, Me."

❸ See to it that your partner has time to indulge in her favorite pastime or workout by running an undesirable errand for her. As George Eliot wrote, "What do we live for, if not to make life less difficult for each other?"

Day 13

GOD WANTS YOU TO:
Be Confident in Who You Are

"In him and through faith in him we may approach
God with freedom and confidence."
Ephesians 3:12

Reclaim your sense of self

Russian-American novelist Ayn Rand once quipped, "To
say 'I love you' one must first be able to say the 'I.'" It is
true that it is impossible to love someone else if you do not
love yourself. But loving yourself was easier when you and
your husband had less responsibilities and more fun. It was
also easier when you and your wife were in the throes of
courtship, and you were constantly hearing from her you
were good-looking, interesting, and smart.

But when the family always comes first, compromise becomes
a way of life. As a result, your own interests tend to suffer.
As your sense of self is buried beneath the needs of one's
family, your confidence takes a dive, because you no longer
remember how it feels to assert your own needs.

Be assertive, not aggressive

Assertiveness is a key component of self-esteem, but too many people confuse assertiveness with aggression as they struggle to reclaim their independence. Learn to restore your sense of self without becoming aggressive toward your partner. Assertive people are decisive and confident. They are able to communicate their needs without trampling others' feelings. Their quiet power comes from being self-assured and grounded in their individuality. Aggressive people, on the other hand, are usually unable to express themselves well. They resort to mean-spirited or brutish tactics to further their own agendas. Avoid using aggressive tactics in your marriage. Assertiveness is a far more effective way to recover your individuality. Use the following scenario to guide you toward a more assertive personality:

Scenario: Your partner has a big project due at work. She warns you that she won't be able to do any housework until it is done. But you yourself have to prepare a presentation for an important client and don't have time to do additional chores. You earn more money that your partner and think your presentation is more important than her project. Without fighting, you want to impart to your spouse that your presentation requires as much time to prepare as hers.

Aggressive response: "I make more money than you do, so my presentation is more important. You'll have to work around my schedule, not the other way around."

Assertive response: "I also have important work due this week, so I can't take on any extra chores. Let's consider getting a house cleaner this week so we can both focus on our work."

YOUR DAILY | Act of Love

Today, avoid commenting on your weaknesses. When you highlight your negative qualities, it repels your spouse instead of drawing her closer. Remember, insecurity is major a turn-off. Put an end to statements like, "I wish I was younger/thinner/smarter/richer/more successful." Such comments reflect a poor attitude and actually encourage your partner to view you as weak and self-loathing—two very unattractive qualities.

DATE ACCOMPLISHED: ....

DAILY REFLECTIONS: Write down whether you tend to seek consensus before making decisions. Note how easily you are dissuaded from having your own opinions. Assess how often you think bad thoughts about yourself. Finally, rate your self-confidence on a scale of 1 to 10.

....

....

....

....

....

....

....

....

ADDITIONAL WAYS
to improve your marriage

Combat insecurity as if your life depends on it—because it just might. Low-self esteem leads to depression and anger, both of which can cause high blood pressure, an irregular heartbeat, and a weakened immune system. Low self-esteem also results in lethargy, apathy, and poor hygiene, all of which make you look and feel your worst.

You owe it to yourself, to your partner, and even to God to be as healthy and happy as possible. Take steps to boost your self-confidence by cultivating a healthy lifestyle. Exercise regularly, and eat a high-fiber, low-fat diet that includes several servings of fresh fruits and vegetables. Limit fast-food and junk-food intake as such binges often result in remorse and feeling bad about oneself. Finally, make efforts to dress and look your best. Take note of how feeling better about yourself translates into more positive relationships with the people around you, and especially your spouse.

3 exercises to help you incorporate today's theme

❶ Repeat the following affirmation in front of a mirror: "I am a confident, capable, and lovable person."

❷ Say "no" when you are uncomfortable with a request or feel stretched too thin to commit to an event. Don't justify your answer; just say it with confidence.

❸ Make a list of your best qualities and keep it in your purse or wallet. Read it to yourself when insecurity creeps in.

Day 14

GOD WANTS YOU TO:
Keep Good Company

"Do not be misled.
'Bad company corrupts good character.'"
1 Corinthians 15:33

Choose friends who bring out the best in you

Many disagreements between couples arise because of outside influences or the company the other keeps. Who are your friends and what do they say about you? Do they fit the description of friendship outlined by William Penn, who 400 years ago wrote, "A true friend unbosoms freely, advises justly, assists readily, adventures boldly, takes all patiently, defends courageously, and continues a friend unchangeably"? If so, then you keep good company. It is likely that your friends share your values and are a true reflection of your character and good judgment. However, if your partner finds fault among your friends, there could be a problem. Think carefully about the people you spend the most time with, and evaluate whether they inspire your best or worst qualities.

DAY

14

Use the following list as a guide to evaluate your friendships. Fill in the blank spots with your friends' names:

- I often regret my behavior after spending time with _____ _____.
- I always drink/smoke/eat too much when I go out with _____.
- I cringe every time _____ opens his/her mouth.
- My partner wishes I would not spend time with _____.
- I am proud of my friendship with _____.
- I trust _____ completely.
- Though we sometimes disagree, _____ is always respectful when s/he expresses his/her opinion.

Don't be afraid to move on

Many of us get stuck in friendships with people from our past. Though presently we have little in common, a shared history keeps us connected. These are the folks that often cause the most grief in marriages. Though you admit you get very little out of these friendships, you are reluctant to choose your spouse over an old friend. By making the decision to move on, however, you also choose to honor God's will. Remember that He, like your spouse, asks that you avoid bad company and keep your good character intact.

Make new friends

Use your connections at work or church to make new friends who fit your current lifestyle. Consider joining a social group that shares similar interests and hobbies. But remember that Proverbs 12:26 declares, "A righteous man is cautious in friendship." Take time to get to know new acquaintances before you forge a deeper connection.

YOUR DAILY | Act of Love

Turn down a social invitation from a friend whom
your partner dislikes. Do not resent having to say
"no." Rather, view it as an act of faith in your partner's
judgment in people. Use your night in to discuss your
spouse's feelings about this particular friend. Never
threaten to choose your friend over your
spouse—even when you are angry.

DATE ACCOMPLISHED: ....

DAILY REFLECTIONS: Write about whether your friends
share your core values. What do you do or talk about with
your friends that reflects these values? Explore how cutting
ties with those who encourage bad behavior might improve
your marriage.

....

....

....

....

....

....

....

....

ADDITIONAL WAYS
to improve your marriage

Everyone needs time to bond with friends of their own gender. Remember what author C.S. Lewis once expressed: "Friendship is born at that moment when one person says to another, 'What! You too? I thought I was the only one!'" Besides, socializing without your spouse now and then is an important way to preserve your individuality. With all of this in mind, encourage your partner to have friends outside of your relationship. Urge him or her to enjoy a visit with good friends whenever possible. Do not resent the time she spends away from you and, likewise, avoid feeling jealous about his night out with the guys.

3 exercises to help you incorporate today's theme

❶ Make a list of the people in your life who share your values.

❷ Distance yourself from friends who have a negative impact on your life. Start by not returning emails, text messages, or phone calls as frequently as you used to.

❸ Join a social group, athletic class, or club that includes interests that match your current lifestyle.

Day 15

GOD WANTS YOU TO:
Apologize Without Being Asked

"He who conceals his sins does
not prosper, but whoever confesses and
renounces them finds mercy."

Proverbs 28:13

Explain what happened

An effective apology takes finesse, attention to detail, and the ability to set aside your pride. It is a carefully crafted statement that must be delivered artfully and in stages. The first step is to recount what happened. This ensures you and your spouse are on the same page about the problem. It also affords you the opportunity to tell your side of the story. Avoid blaming or judging your partner during your explanation. Simply state the facts as you experienced them and move on to the next step.

Take responsibility for your actions

The second step is to accept responsibility for your role in the conflict without justifying or defending your actions. Keep statements short and to the point. Allow your partner to vent her anger or to express how badly you hurt his feelings. Stick with the present situation and avoid bringing up examples of similar occasions in which your partner did the same thing to you. Never bring up unrelated issues or past grievances.

Express regret

Finally, statements of regret are the backbone of your apology and also make up the third step of the process. How your partner receives yours depends on how it is delivered. There is a right way and a wrong way to say, "I'm sorry."

An effective apology includes all of the following components:
- Being genuine
- Choosing your words carefully
- Making sure your facial expressions match your tone
- Maintaining eye contact
- Stating why you are sorry. For example, "I am so sorry that I was late to pick you up at the airport!"

Prevent a botched apology by avoiding these phrases:
- "I'm sorry, but..."
- "I couldn't help it!"
- "It wasn't my fault!"
- "It's your fault!"
- "You forced me to say/do that!"
- "I'm sorry I'm not as perfect as you!"
- "You're overreacting."

YOUR DAILY | Act of Love

Today, make it a point to hold yourself accountable for any recent offences against your spouse. Issue a genuine apology before your partner asks for one, and do not expect immediate forgiveness. It may be difficult to humble yourself, but a heartfelt apology is the first step toward reconciliation. Increase the impact of your apology by delivering it in writing.

DATE ACCOMPLISHED: ....

DAILY REFLECTIONS: Write a few sentences on why it is difficult for you to apologize to your partner. Is it because you do not want to admit you were wrong? Is it because you truly do not think you were wrong? Or, does apologizing make you feel vulnerable?

....

....

....

....

....

....

....

....

ADDITIONAL WAYS
to improve your marriage

Drive your apology home by following it up with a gift. Within two days of apologizing to your spouse, give a small present to let him or her know you still take the situation seriously. Have flowers, a favorite food, a book, or another small, personal token ready to give to your spouse. The gift should be modest in price and be more about the thought involved than the item itself. Consider the present not as buying your partner's affections but rather as an extension of your apology.

Don't repeat your mistake

How seriously your partner takes your apology depends on your history. If you have a habit of repeatedly apologizing for the same thing, chances are your partner will take your penitence with a grain of salt. So mean it when you say, "It won't happen again." On the other hand, if you know it will happen again, do not promise it won't. Rather, work with your spouse to find a way around the conflict.

3 exercises to help you incorporate today's theme

❶ Make up a silly apology song and sing it to your spouse.

❷ Bake an apology cake and ask your spouse to forgive you after he or she blows out the candles.

❸ Practice your apology in front of a mirror until the words roll off your tongue with sincerity and ease.

Day 16

GOD WANTS YOU TO:
Let Go of Angry Feelings

"You do not stay angry forever
but delight to show mercy. You will
again have compassion on us."
Micah 7:18-19

Explore why you are angry

Anger can come on very fast and hang around for as long as we let it. In some cases it lingers indefinitely, to the point where we can't recall what even made us so mad in the first place. Prolonged anger negatively affects our overall demeanor and outlook, and because it causes us to hold grudges, feel resentful, and endure depression, is our most destructive emotion. Avoid the more damaging consequences of anger by dealing with it when it strikes. Think about the following:

- What are you angry about?
- When did you become angry?

- How do you deal with anger?
- Why are you still angry?
- With whom are you angry?

Free yourself from resentment

It may feel as though you punish your spouse when you stay angry but, in reality, such animosity only hurts you. When anger turns into resentment and grudge-holding, you eventually become cynical and unhappy. Left unchecked, cynicism, resentment, and rage will cause you to become a miserable and lonely person. Free yourself from this fate by incorporating the following into your lifestyle:

- Immediately deal with the source of your anger.
- Tell your spouse when you are angry.
- Be specific about what made you mad.
- Ask for an apology.
- Write about your feelings.
- Rate your anger on a scale from 1 to 10 each day.

Embrace forgiveness

Refusal to forgive your partner can permanently harm your relationship. Grudges force couples to drift apart, and the longer one is held, the more difficult it is to get close again. Remember that God wants us to forgive each other for all wrongdoings, regardless of how difficult it may be. Ephesians 4:26 reminds us to forgive each other quickly: "Do not let the sun go down while you are still angry."

YOUR DAILY | Act of Love

Let anger flow through you today without allowing it
spill over into your interactions with your partner.
Too often we allow minor annoyances to build up and
to turn into angry outbursts. On this day, though, give
your anger to God in prayer instead of unleashing
it on your partner. Excuse yourself, take five deep
breaths, and ask God for peace. Pray
for as long as it takes you to calm down.

DATE ACCOMPLISHED: ....

DAILY REFLECTIONS: List any grudges you harbor against
your spouse. Consider why you hang on to them. How does
it serve you to stay angry, and how would it benefit your
marriage to let them go?

....
....
....
....
....
....
....
....

ADDITIONAL WAYS
to improve your marriage

Extreme stress, depression, substance abuse, and other factors may prevent some people from being able to control their anger. In such cases anger management classes may be necessary. Classes are designed to teach you how to process stressors that cause anger. You will be taught how to control angry outbursts and learn anger-redirection techniques. You will also learn to recognize when rage has the potential to become dangerous. Instructors give you the tools to effectively communicate and manage stress so that you never go from mad to violent. Finally, you will acquire a valuable support system to call upon when you are at-risk for expressing anger in unhealthy ways.

When you are able to let go of anger, you will not only be in a better mood but in better health as well. In fact, the Mayo Clinic reports that forgiving others may yield the following health benefits: lowered blood pressure, decreased heart rate, less risk for substance abuse, fewer symptoms of depression and anxiety, and reduced chronic pain.

3 exercises to help you incorporate today's theme

❶ When you fear you might lose control of your temper, leave the situation. Do 10 jumping jacks and then count to 100.

❷ Meditate for 15-30 minutes every morning and before bed.

❸ Take several deep breaths before responding to emails, text messages, or other forms of communication when you are upset.

Day 17

GOD WANTS YOU TO:
Be Joyful in Your Love

"Be joyful always; pray continually;
give thanks in all circumstances, for this is
God's will for you in Christ Jesus."

1 Thessalonians 5:16-18

Try something new together

Every couple ends up into a routine-induced rut now and
then. It does not mean anything is wrong, per se, unless
the rut becomes your status quo. When people are bored
they become lazy, short-tempered, and ill at ease with each
other. But there is no room for joy in such a moody house!
The remedy for a cranky home, therefore, is to reintroduce
spontaneity into your married life.

Spontaneous acts of joy revitalize passion, rekindle romance,
and remind you of why you married your partner. Revive joy
in your marriage by surprising your partner with something
new, such as:

• After eating dinner in a restaurant, drive your spouse

to a fancy dessert cafe or a hotel instead of going home.
- Take a long drive together without a destination in mind.
- Choose which movie to see when you get to the theater, rather than in advance.
- Wake your partner up to watch the sunrise.
- Call in sick to work and spend the day together.

Stay healthy and attractive

Fernando, Billy Crystal's character on *Saturday Night Live*, used to say, "It is better to look good than to feel good." In many ways, Fernando was right. Your appearance directly impacts how you feel about yourself. If you wear old, baggy sweatpants to bed every night you will not feel very sexy or spontaneous. But throw on a pair of tailored pajamas or a sexy nightie and you immediately feel brand new. Dressing up for your partner is a quick and easy way to bring joy and energy back into your marriage.

Fernando's catch phrase is equally true in reverse. That is, "It is better to feel good than to look good." In other words, even if you are of the proper weight and have a nice haircut, an unhealthy lifestyle will leave you with little energy to devote to your marriage. However, a balanced diet paired with regular exercise boosts your energy level and improves your mood. Then, you are in a much better position to bring spontaneity and joy into your relationship.

YOUR DAILY | Act of Love

Express only joyful sentiments today, especially when it comes to comments regarding your partner or your marriage. Ignore the urge to complain and make positive statements throughout the day. These can include things like, "I am proud to be your partner" or "I had a wonderful day with you." Your spouse will appreciate a break from your usual grumbling and be pleasantly surprised by your new attitude.

DATE ACCOMPLISHED: ....

DAILY REFLECTIONS: Write down each time you complain about something. Make note of your mood when you complain and whether you feel better afterwards. Do the same for each joyful statement you make.

....

....

....

....

....

....

....

....

ADDITIONAL WAYS
to improve your marriage

Fight the urge to say something negative whenever it strikes. Mull over the thought before you say it out loud. Consider whether it is something that actually needs to be expressed or if it is just something to say. If the latter is true, find a way to spin it into a positive declaration. For example, instead of criticizing how your partner drives, say something nice about the scenery. Spin all of your complaints into affirmations for at least one week and keep a record of the experience. Note how often you have to flip your thoughts before you speak.

Finally, celebrate at least one thing with your partner every day. Propose a toast during dinner, share a decadent dessert, or congratulate each other for being great parents. Acknowledge every small win and delight in the small everyday accomplishments that together add up to the great successes of life.

3 exercises to help you incorporate today's theme

❶ Brighten up the house with fresh flowers and music. Dance around the room with your partner instead of plopping down in front of the TV.

❷ Surprise your spouse by filling your bedroom with flowers or balloons.

❸ Burn a CD of your favorite upbeat songs and put it in your spouse's car. It will pep up his or her morning commute!

Day 18

GOD WANTS YOU TO:
Make Your Partner Laugh

"He will yet fill your mouth with laughter
and your lips with shouts of joy."
Job 8:21

Surprise your partner with random acts of humor
Nothing feels as good as a deep laugh shared with someone
you love. Today, aim to catch your partner off-guard by
saying or doing something funny when he or she least expects
it. This requires you to be on the lookout for situational
humor. When you see something funny happen, comment
on it immediately. Do not wait to share your witticism until
you are able to polish your delivery. Since much humor lies
in the element of surprise, use guerilla tactics to make him
laugh as soon as you notice something is funny. Blurt out
whatever thought comes to mind as soon as it comes to you.
Focus on taking advantage of the moment, and don't worry
about censoring yourself or sounding dumb.

Use props
Popular comedians Carrot Top and Gallagher use props to

make their audiences laugh hysterically. Crowds go wild when Gallagher smashes a watermelon with a sledgehammer or when Carrot Top pulls a prop from a trunk, nails a one-liner, and tosses it aside. You, too, can become a prop comic using objects from your own home to make your partner laugh. Some ideas for prop comedy include:

- Use a banana to "answer" the phone.
- Walk around the house wearing one of your partner's outfits and pretend like nothing is different.
- Put on a tiny hat.
- Wear your bathing suit over your clothes.
- Use a spatula as a cane.

Integrate kids and pets into your humor

The creators of the television shows *Kids Say the Darndest Things*, *America's Funniest Home Videos*, and *The Planet's Funniest Pets* know that kids and pets provide comedy gold. Use your children's antics and your pet's tricks to make your partner laugh. The following suggestions will help you incorporate them into your comedy routine:

- Let your toddler choose what everyone eats for dinner.
- Teach your dog to walk on two legs.
- Put a bow tie on your pet's collar.
- Dress your pet up in a superhero costume.
- Throw a ball and tell the cat to fetch it.

Keep your jokes above the belt

It is one thing to use yourself as a punch line, but don't make fun of your partner or others just to get a laugh. Jokes at the expense of others come off as mean-spirited and desperate.

YOUR DAILY | Act of Love

Get your spouse to laugh at something at least once today, because laughter decreases stress and increases intimacy. Share an old high school photo, clip an amusing comic strip and leave it next to his coffee cup, imitate her favorite celebrity, make up a silly song about your kids or pets, or read hilarious headlines from TheOnion.com out loud.

DATE ACCOMPLISHED: ....

DAILY REFLECTIONS: Do you remember the last time you and your spouse laughed together? What was so funny? Write down how it felt to share this hilarious moment with your partner.

....

....

....

....

....

....

....

....

ADDITIONAL WAYS
to improve your marriage

Nineteenth century social reformer Henry Ward Beecher once wrote, "Mirth is God's medicine. Everybody ought to bathe in it." Indeed, God wants you to be full of mirth, joy, and happiness, especially in your faith. Find laughter together in the Word. Use teamwork to make Bible study groups and church functions sparkle with humor. Plan fundraisers that include funniest hat/yearbook photo/fake mustache contests; host an ugly Christmas sweater potluck; and encourage your pastor or priest to tell a few jokes at the next service. Let how you worship reflect the great joy you feel whenever you praise God.

3 exercises to help you incorporate today's theme

❶ Go with your partner to a local comedy club.

❷ Share a humorous story from your day with your partner—even if it is embarrassing and your behavior or words are the punch line.

❸ Email your partner a funny video of the day from YouTube.com.

Day 19

GOD WANTS YOU TO:
Exercise Control with Food and Drink

"Be wise, and keep your heart on the right path. Do not join those who drink too much wine or gorge themselves on meat, for drunkards and gluttons become poor, and drowsiness clothes them in rags."

Proverbs 23:19-21

Treat your body like a temple

God gave your body to you as a gift. It is His unique, one-of-a-kind creation, and it is your responsibility to treat it as a Holy vessel. 1 Corinthians 6:19 begs the question, "Do you not know that your body is a temple of the Holy Spirit, who is in you, whom you have received from God?" But when you regularly engage in gluttonous behavior, you poison your body and insult God's creation.

This does not mean it is never OK to indulge in guilty-pleasure food and drink—it is. But reserve your enjoyment of decadent treats and alcoholic drinks for special occasions.

They taste better when consumed less frequently, and such indulgences also serve as rewards when doled out sparingly.

Avoid the damaging effects of alcohol
Alcohol consumption is only acceptable when you are able to limit how much you drink. The U.S. Department of Health and Human Services issued an "Alcohol Alert" in 2004 which warned of the following effects alcohol has on the brain:

Short-term effects:
- Trouble walking and maintaining balance
- Blurred vision
- Memory impairment
- Slow reaction time
- Slurred speech
- Blackouts

Long-term effects:
- Brain shrinkage
- Permanent memory loss
- Thiamine deficiency (necessary for brain function)
- Confusion
- Lack of muscle control
- Inability to generate new brain cells

Alcohol effects our personalities, too. Sometimes, people who drink become overly emotional or unduly argumentative. In these states, couples already at odds with one another are likely to let small disagreements erupt into major schisms. With this in mind, it is best to put alcohol aside, especially when your marriage is going through a rocky period.

YOUR DAILY | Act of Love

Today, make a promise to God and your partner that you will take care of your body. Vow to have no more than one glass of wine or beer with dinner, and abstain from drinking hard alcohol. Pledge to exercise portion control and to snack on fresh fruits and vegetables instead of pre-packaged junk food. Plan meals for the week, and avoid fast food. Promise to exercise regularly and to treat your body as the holy vessel it is.

DATE ACCOMPLISHED: ....

DAILY REFLECTIONS: Keep a food diary to get a handle on your eating habits. Write down everything you eat or drink. Include the size of the portions and the time of consumption.

....

....

....

....

....

....

....

....

ADDITIONAL WAYS
to improve your marriage

People gravitate toward what is easiest. So if your pantry is stocked with sweet and salty snacks, and there is always cold beer in your refrigerator, that is what you will eat and drink. Make it easier to resist unhealthy choices by not stocking your kitchen with junk food and alcohol. Fill the pantry with whole grain crackers, breads, natural peanut butter, and pasta. Load up the fridge with fresh fruits and vegetables, yogurt, hummus, and low-fat cheese. Drink herbal iced tea and water with lemon or cucumber slices. Be creative and snack smart!

Be well for your family

Use your family as motivation to make smart decisions in your diet and in your lifestyle. Literally imagine how the next drink or the order of super-sized French fries might shorten your lifespan. In turn, let your healthy choices be a shining example of moderation to your spouse and children. Use each meal as an opportunity to teach your children to feed their mind and bodies in healthy moderation. Never let them see you eat or drink too much, because children will mimic their parents' behaviors.

3 exercises to help you incorporate today's theme

❶ Have no more than 2 drinks when you go out with friends.

❷ Eat a salad or cup of soup before meals to prevent becoming too hungry and overeating.

❸ Eat six small meals a day instead of three large ones to keep your blood sugar stable and your metabolism working.

Day 20

GOD WANTS YOU TO:

Be Courteous to Your Partner

"Live in harmony with one another;
be sympathetic, love as brothers, be
compassionate and humble. Do not repay
evil with evil or insult with insult,
but with blessing."
1 Peter 3:8-9

Treat your partner respectfully
1 Peter 2:17 reminds us, "Show proper respect to everyone."
And above all, the most important person to treat respectfully
is your partner. Showing proper respect means that even
when under great stress, you will resist the temptation to be
short-tempered or snotty with your spouse. Never call him
names or belittle her in front of your friends. Be consistently
positive when you speak about your relationship to others,
and discuss marital problems with your partner first.

Interestingly, some couples think it is enough to treat their
partner respectfully in public. But it is how you treat your

partner in private that really reflects how you feel about him or her. With this in mind, make your private interactions as respectful as your public ones. Think of how you would feel if someone overheard you talk down to your wife or belittle your husband. If you wouldn't say it in front of someone else, don't say it to your partner in private. In addition:

- Don't interrupt your wife while she is speaking.
- Avoid speaking for your husband.
- Do not make jokes at your partner's expense.
- Never insult your partner's intelligence.

Exhibit good manners

With email and text messages at the forefront of modern communication, slang and shorthand have become more common than ever before. As a result, good manners and proper etiquette are a dying art. "Yes, sir" and "No, ma'am" have fallen by the wayside, and some couples go weeks without ever saying "thank you" to each other. But when you drop verbal expressions of kindness and gratitude from your vocabulary, it indicates that you take your partner for granted.

Ms. Manners would advise you to invoke certain conversational formalities whenever you speak to your spouse. Always say "Please, thank you, you're welcome" and "excuse me." If these feel too formal for your style, come up with your own set of pleasantries that you repeat often. Don't let a day go by without bidding your partner a "good morning" or "goodnight." Interactions that include such niceties highlight the level of respect you have for your spouse. They also elevate expectations for how you speak to each other.

YOUR DAILY | Act of Love

Recapture the spirit of the early days of your relationship, and show your spouse that you still care enough to woo her. Dedicate today to performing chivalrous acts. Open doors, pull out chairs, take her coat, hold his hand, and defer to your partner in conversation. For added effect, use terms of endearment in conversation, such as dear or honey.

DATE ACCOMPLISHED: ....

DAILY REFLECTIONS: Write a brief paragraph about what you did to keep your spouse interested when you first started dating. Include actions that inspired courteous behavior, and note how things have changed.

....
....
....
....
....
....
....
....

ADDITIONAL WAYS
to improve your marriage

Speak only kind, supportive words about your spouse to friends and family, and take your concerns directly to your partner. In other words, do not smile at your partner, and say, "yes dear," then turn to your friend and roll your eyes. It may seem funny, but it is a clear sign of disrespect. Additionally, never speak poorly of your spouse to your children—even in jest. Statements like, "Mommy's crazy!" or "Your father is a cheapskate!" have a strong influence on how your child views your partner—as well as their opinion of you.

Indeed, children learn to be adults by watching their parents. Boys learn how to treat women by watching how their father treats their mother; girls figure out what kind of man makes a good partner by internalizing their mother's relationship with their dad. Thus, every word you speak to your partner in front of your children impacts how they learn these lessons. Tone, body language, and facial expressions all contribute to how kids perceive relationships between adults. Show them the best possible version of your marriage by being kind, affectionate, attentive, and respectful to your partner at all times.

3 exercises to help you incorporate today's theme

❶ Ask, "Can I get you anything?" whenever you are about to leave the room or go shopping.

❷ Wait for your partner to be seated before eating.

❸ Let your partner enter a room first.

Day 21

GOD WANTS YOU TO:
Tame Your Tongue

"With the tongue we praise our Lord and Father,
and with it we curse men, who have been made in
God's likeness. Out of the same mouth come praise
and cursing. My brothers, this should not be. Can
both fresh water and salt water flow from
the same spring?"

James 3:9-11

Recognize your danger zone

In truth, you have to want to avoid saying something mean
to your spouse. Help yourself want to become a nicer, more
compassionate partner by getting yourself into a calm state
when you are most agitated. Recognize the physical signs
that indicate your frustration has mounted to a dangerous
level. These include:

- Rapid heartbeat
- Flushed cheeks, neck, or chest
- Tension in the jaw, neck, shoulders, and back
- Clenched fists

- Bulging eyes
- Pursed lips

If you experience any of these symptoms, you are at risk to snap at your spouse. Take several deep breaths and excuse yourself from the argument. Revisit the conversation later after you have regained your ability to be civil.

Pretend you are wearing a microphone

Everyone is on their best behavior when they are watched by others—especially when they are angry. For example, parents rarely have tirades in public, where they are more likely to use low tones to discipline their children. Use this principle in the more frustrating moments with your spouse. Pretend there is a microphone clipped to your shirt when you talk to your husband or wife. Act as though every word you speak is broadcast to a large audience who will judge you harshly if you say anything unkind. Imagine, also, that a giant APPLAUSE sign lights up whenever you control your temper and tame your tongue.

Consider the consequences

Perhaps you bite your tongue every time your partner does something annoying. After a while, the temptation to scream, "Stop doing that, you idiot!" may feel impossible to fight. In the moment, it might even feel good to let your spouse have it. But think of the consequences of calling your partner a mean name. You may cause permanent damage to your relationship, irreparably hurt your husband's feelings, bruise your wife's ego, or break your partner's trust. As novelist Joseph Conrad warned, "A word carries far—very far—deals destruction through time as the bullets go flying through space."

YOUR DAILY | Act of Love

Make today's mantra, "Be nice or be quiet." Literally
bite your tongue to avoid making sarcastic, rude, or
negative comments to your spouse. Put your hand over
your mouth or bite the inside of your cheek as an added
reminder to think before you speak. Remember that
you cannot take hurtful words back
once they are spoken aloud.

DATE ACCOMPLISHED: ....

DAILY REFLECTIONS: Do you ever say hurtful things to
your partner on purpose? If so, write why. Is it that you want
to make him feel horrible? Are you trying to show her just
how angry you are? Get to the root of this problem through
your writing.

....

....

....

....

....

....

....

....

ADDITIONAL WAYS
to improve your marriage

Use the power of speech (or silence) to remain supportive and loving to your partner—especially when he is at his most vulnerable. Your marriage is your best friendship and must be protected from harmful and hateful speech. Proverbs 16:28 warns, "A gossip separates close friends." Do not spread rumors about your partner, nor belittle her in anger or to show off. Keep important news close and only share it with your spouse's permission. Always defend your spouse to others, and put up a united front even when you disagree with your partner's actions. Finally, never broadcast your partner's mood or personal problems to friends without his or her knowledge or permission.

3 exercises to help you incorporate today's theme

❶ Save an angrily composed email as a draft. Wait a full hour before returning to it, and then decide if you still want to send it.

❷ Remove yourself from a heated argument. Go for a walk around the block or take a hot shower—do whatever it takes to calm down so you do not say something nasty to your spouse.

❸ Agree to a list of words that are not acceptable to say to each other under any circumstances.

Day 22

GOD WANTS YOU TO:
Be Honorable with Your Intentions

"Rid yourselves of all malice and all deceit,
hypocrisy, envy, and slander of every kind."
1 Peter 2:1

Always tell the truth

Your marriage was founded on the assumption that you
would always be truthful with your partner. In this endeavor,
remember that the honorable person tells the whole story,
even when it reflects poorly on him. In times when it is scary
to tell the truth, gain strength from Psalm 43:3, which asks
of God, "Send forth your light and your truth, let them
guide me." Include this phrase in your prayers when you
find yourself asking God to guide you toward doing the
right thing. Deliver the truth honorably when you have done
something wrong, and avoid the following tricks:

- Do not leave out details or water down the truth to
  soften the blow.
- Never transfer blame onto someone else.
- Avoid speaking in such general or confusing terms that

your partner cannot follow the story.
- Do not exaggerate, downplay, or alter the facts.

Develop a reputation for dependability

Be someone your spouse can count on in both times of crisis and normal day-to-day events. A basic requirement is to stick around for emergencies and to show up to every function you commit to—including all school happenings, sports games, recitals, social engagements, church meetings, and counseling sessions. It is anything but honorable to forget a special event and disappoint your family. So, set an example of responsibility that others seek to emulate. Live as if you expect God to interview everyone you know to learn about your character. With every decision you make and action you take, imagine that God will ask your peers, "Was he or she dependable?"

Live according to your principles

Billionaire John Templeton once said, "High ethics and religious principles form the basis for success and happiness in every area of life." Certainly, ethical behavior and adherence to your faith will help you make principled decisions.

Some tips for living according to your principles include:

- Say what you mean, and mean what you say.
- Work hard.
- Give due credit to others.
- Never compromise your integrity.
- Worship as your faith dictates.
- Take responsibility for both accomplishments and mistakes.
- Accept and apply constructive criticism.

YOUR DAILY | Act of Love

Use today to judge your honorability by evaluating whether your actions match your motives. For example, do not compliment your spouse only to prevent him from noticing that you forgot to pay a bill. A better way to handle the situation is to tell your spouse you did not pay it and hold the compliment for when you really mean it.

DATE ACCOMPLISHED: ....

DAILY REFLECTIONS: Write a few sentences about why it is important in a marriage for both partners to be honorable. Is your spouse an honorable person? Do you believe that you live according to your principles?

....

....

....

....

....

....

....

....

ADDITIONAL WAYS
to improve your marriage

Enlist the help of a couple both you and your spouse respect to act as your mentors. Turn to them when you need guidance to act honorably and according to your principles. As Proverbs 12:15 plainly states, "The way of a fool is right in his own eyes, but a wise man is he who listens to counsel." Choose a couple who has a relationship you admire, one that is based on values and qualities you yourself want your marriage to possess. Preferably, the couple will have been married for at least 5 years longer than you have been and have weathered a significant challenge together. This couple should make you and your spouse want to be better people whenever you are around them.

3 exercises to help you incorporate today's theme

❶ Never boast about committing good deeds or acts of kindness.

❷ Keep a "Diary of Intentions" and note when your actions support or contradict your motives.

❸ Tell your partner the hardest truth first.

Day 23

Stick to Your Values

"Anyone who listens to the Word but does not do what it says is like a man who looks at his face in a mirror and, after looking at himself, goes away and immediately forgets what he looks like. But the man who looks intently into the perfect law... he will be blessed in what he does."

James 1:23-25

Define your values and standards

Values are the standards by which you base all of your decisions and actions. They are influenced by your religion, upbringing, education, geographical location, social affiliations, and interests. Your goal is to define a set of values that fits you based on those influences. Choose values that reflect the partner you aspire to be.

Once you select your values, create a code of conduct around 5 of the most important of them. The values you choose should be general enough that you can apply them to any situation. For example, if the value you select is "compassion," the corresponding code of conduct might be, "I will treat others compassionately, especially my partner." Other values you might select are acceptance, appreciation, faith, truth, and humility. Prioritize your list and think about how to incorporate your newly defined values into your relationship with your partner.

Evaluate your current lifestyle

The next step is to evaluate whether you live up to these values. Consider how your profession, relationships, social life, hobbies, and interests support—or contradict—your standards. Admit to all areas in which you fall short of living up to your principles. For example, if "family" is at the top of your list but you consistently work 80 hours a week, you must cut down on your hours to live up to this value.

Take action

Make sure your words, actions, and behaviors advertise you as a person that sticks to his or her values. Be consistent, and use your code of conduct as a tool to make conscious choices that support your priorities. Pull out your list of principles to live by whenever decision-making opportunities arise. For example, compare the responsibilities of a new job offer with your values and see if they match before you accept it.

Be patient

Be patient as you wait for sticking to your values to positively impact your marriage. Things you can expect to experience:

- Your spouse will be proud of the "new you."
- You will have a clean conscience.
- Your life will have purpose.

YOUR DAILY | Act of Love

Write down the top 5 qualities you value most and rank them in order of importance. Your list should include characteristics that exemplify your values. It might look something like this: Loyalty, responsibility, honesty, faithfulness, and industriousness. Next to each of these, write ways in which your partner exhibits each of these qualities. Use clear, specific examples, and share them with your spouse.

DATE ACCOMPLISHED: ....

DAILY REFLECTIONS: Jot down ways in which your lifestyle supports your value system. Do you ever feel forced to compromise your beliefs? Does your spouse share your code of conduct? What values were important to you 5 years ago, and which do you think will be important 5 years from now?

....

....

....

....

....

....

....

....

ADDITIONAL WAYS

to improve your marriage

Create a personal mission statement that inspires you to stick to your core values. Use your list of principles to craft a paragraph that begins with the person you are now and ends with who you want to become. Include specific, action-oriented steps that simultaneously express your goals and support your value system. Focus on realistic achievements that force you to step outside your comfort zone, but avoid setting unreasonable goals that you know you cannot achieve. Include ways to be a better partner in your mission statement, and share the polished version with your spouse.

3 exercises to help you incorporate today's theme

❶ Select 3 passages from the Bible that best support your core values. Copy them down in your journal or in this book, and internalize their meaning.

❷ Purchase or create a piece of art that inspires you to stick to your values. Hang it in a prominent place in your home to remind you of the significance these values have in crafting the relationship you have with yourself, your spouse, and everyone else in your life.

❸ Ask your partner to comment on whether your life together reflects his or her values.

Day 24

GOD WANTS YOU TO:
Encourage Your Partner's Talents

"Encourage one another and build each other up."
1 Thessalonians 5:11

Come to terms with your partner's individuality
Think about what attracted you to your partner before he became your spouse. Most likely, you were drawn to his or her creativity and independent spirit. When you were dating these qualities were irresistible, and they inspired passion and pursuit. Now that you are married, however, perhaps qualities like creativity and independence seem threatening. This misperception is a fatal flaw in the logic of an insecure spouse. The true threat to your relationship comes not from encouraging creative independence, but in oppressing it.

Trust that when you give your spouse room to express herself, she will recycle her creative energy back into your relationship. Indeed, it will dramatically improve your marriage to praise your partner's creative side. Your partner will feel supported and acknowledged as a talented individual. He or she will be generally happier, which will translate into increased satisfaction at home. The small annoyances of domestic life won't matter as much in contrast with your great generosity and support.

Ask your partner, "What can I do?"

It is OK if you are unsure how to support your partner's talents. Perhaps, you do not have any free time to take on extra responsibilities, or you disapprove of or can't connect with your partner's method of creative expression. Regardless of time constraints or your opinion of your partner's pursuits, there is always one thing you can do: Ask your partner what you can do to help him or her realize any creative goals. Request specific, realistic examples of ways you can encourage your spouse. Only commit to implementing ideas that are reasonable, and be consistent with your follow-through.

Ways to support your spouse's creative endeavors include:

- Allot your partner one chore-free night a week to nurture a talent, be it painting, gardening, or rock climbing.
- Email your partner articles, advertisements, and blog posts that apply to her talent.
- Be your partner's first audience. Ask to read her short story or listen to him play a new song.
- Express interest in your partner's progress on a new project.
- Encourage your spouse to revisit an old hobby that used to bring him joy.
- Never tell your spouse his or her talent is a waste of time.
- Offer criticism only when your spouse asks for it.
- Urge your partner to turn his or her hobby into a career.

YOUR DAILY | Act of Love

Today, make it a point to demonstrate to your partner that you value and support his creative pursuits. Come up with a plan to remove obstacles that prevent your spouse from developing her talents. For example, take on extra childcare duties to free him up to play guitar, or create a space in your garage so she can work on her pottery. Even these small efforts show that you respect your partner's talent.

DATE ACCOMPLISHED: ....

DAILY REFLECTIONS: Write down all the talents your partner pursued before you were married. Put a check mark next to those your spouse continues to pursue. Explore how marriage affects time spent nurturing one's creative side.

....

....

....

....

....

....

....

....

ADDITIONAL WAYS
to improve your marriage

One reason you might be threatened by your partner's independent pursuits is because they do not include you. As a result, you may feel left out, ignored, or marginalized by your partner's creative endeavors. Seek out opportunities to support your partner's talents or involve yourself in his or her activities. For example, if your husband plays in a band, take it upon yourself to become band photographer and post photos of his latest performance online. If your wife likes to paint, ask the church to hang her art in their community room or write a blurb about your partner's upcoming project and post it on relevant blogs.

3 exercises to help you incorporate today's theme

❶ Carve out space in your home for a "talent zone." Encourage your spouse to spend time there to nurture his or her talents.

❷ Provide your partner with uninterrupted quiet time a few times a week.

❸ Brag to friends and family about your partner's talents.

Day 25

Always Be Compassionate

"This is what the Lord Almighty says:
'Administer true justice; show mercy and
compassion to one another.'"

Zechariah 7:9

Accept your partner as is

It is difficult to feel compassion when you cannot understand why your partner is a certain way. But it is a mistake to try to change your spouse's personality or preferences to be more like yours. Such attempts put you in opposition to each other instead of on the same side, where you belong. Thus, couples who are unable to accept each other as is lack empathy and become locked in a destructive power struggle.

Put an end to the fight to be right, and invite tolerance and acceptance into your relationship. You will be shocked by how easy it is to treat your partner with compassion once you stop trying to control her and start trying to understand her.

Treat yourself with compassion

In addition to treating your spouse compassionately, practice compassion on yourself. Without this, you will be unable to have empathy for others. Use Psalm 112:4 for inspiration: "Even in darkness light dawns for the upright, for the gracious and compassionate." Be kind to your body and mind, and avoid harsh self-criticisms. Being less critical of yourself will inspire you to be less critical of your partner, too.

Turn to your faith for guidance

Consult the Bible to find examples of compassion. Include your partner in your research and ask to make compassion the theme of your next Bible study. Let God be your mentor as you become familiar with His many acts of compassion—such as the one described in Jonah 3:1 when He spared the Ninevites: "When God saw what they did...he had compassion and did not bring upon them the destruction he had threatened." Even in great anger, God shows compassion. So should you.

Put yourself in your partner's place

The hallmark of compassion is the ability to put yourself in another person's place. Seek to identify with your partner's position by imagining that you are the one with the problem. Appreciate the challenges posed by the situation, and express your desire to help.

YOUR DAILY | Act of Love

Today, listen attentively and avoid trumping your partner's thoughts, feelings, and struggles with your own. Avoid initiating a contest to prove that you have it worse off or that you are under more stress. Regardless of what is going on in your own life, be compassionate about your partner's circumstances. Share applicable stories only when it seems appropriate, and give your spouse your undivided attention.

DATE ACCOMPLISHED: ....

DAILY REFLECTIONS: Write and reflect on times when you could have been more patient and understanding with your partner. Mull over reasons you might be less compassionate toward your partner than you used to be or you should be.

....

....

....

....

....

....

....

....

ADDITIONAL WAYS
to improve your marriage

Practice being compassionate by asking your partner what he or she expects from you before you try to help fix a problem. Oftentimes, your spouse just wants to vent and is not seeking a solution to the problem. Do not try to force your partner to see the brilliance of your ideas or suggestions by repeating them over and over again. It will appear as though you are impatient and more enthralled with your own ideas than with your partner's plight. Realize your partner needs you to be patient, understanding, attentive, and compassionate. Though it can be painful to watch your partner struggle or suffer, sometimes the best thing you can do is listen and be supportive.

3 exercises to help you incorporate today's theme

❶ Send your partner an email that reads, "I'm here for you."

❷ Use phrases such as, "I'm so sorry," "I wish there was something I could do," and "I can see why you are upset!" to express empathy and compassion. Avoid steamrolling your partner's thoughts or completing his or her sentences.

❸ Schedule time to listen to your partner during especially busy weeks.

Day 26

GOD WANTS YOU TO:
Accept, Love, and Appreciate Your Partner's Faults

"Bear with each other and forgive whatever
grievances you may have against one another."

Colossians 3:13

Love unconditionally

On your wedding day you agreed to love your partner unconditionally. Your vows had no caveats to them, such as, "I will love the best parts of you, but complain endlessly about the rest." Of course, it is normal to struggle with your feelings about your spouse's flaws. But when you constantly point out your partner's faults, you violate your promise to love the whole person.

Deuteronomy 6:5 reminds us, "Love the Lord your God with all your heart and with all your soul and with all your strength." Love your partner as completely as you love God.

Indeed, you cannot choose to love certain traits and disregard others. You married a complex individual with moods, habits, behaviors, and patterns of speech that—regardless of how much they annoy you—form your spouse's complete identity.

Recognize your own shortcomings

Learn humility by developing the ability to recognize your own shortcomings. Otherwise, you will find it difficult to overlook your partner's faults. An inflated sense of self often leads to criticism of others, because people who are unable to admit their shortcomings blame others for their problems. Let the following questions help you take an honest look at your behavior. Note any weaknesses that are revealed in your answers. Then work on improving your problem areas instead of focusing on your partner's faults.

- Do you accept responsibility for your part in arguments with your spouse?
- Are you willing to admit when you are wrong?
- Do you blame others when something goes wrong?
- Are you usually/always right?
- Has your partner ever accused you of thinking you are better than everyone else?

Live and let live

Chances are your spouse puts up with many of your faults without complaint. Even though they are frustrating, your partner's quirks are only annoying if you label them as such. Otherwise, he is just a normal person with his own unique set of behaviors and responses—just like you. So try not to micromanage your partner's behavior. Let her make mistakes; embrace his flaws; and allow each other to be yourselves.

YOUR DAILY | Act of Love

Your task today is to allow your partner to be his or her complete self—faults included. Ignore quirks and qualities about your spouse that typically annoy you. Do not comment when he talks with his mouth full or complain about the way she drives. Gather the strength to practice tolerance for behaviors that drive you crazy by asking God for help.

DATE ACCOMPLISHED: ....

DAILY REFLECTIONS: Think about the following excerpt of the Serenity Prayer: "God grant me the serenity to accept the things I cannot change; courage to change the things I can; and wisdom to know the difference." Then, write down at least 3 specific things you want to accept, change, and know the difference between.

....
....
....
....
....
....
....
....

ADDITIONAL WAYS
to improve your marriage

Focusing on your partner's faults makes them nearly impossible to ignore. Try a different tactic. Instead of being hypersensitive to qualities that bother you, acknowledge every action and comment by your spouse that pleases you. Encourage these behaviors with affirmations such as, "I like the way you handled that situation" or, "You are always so organized, it makes grocery shopping go so quickly." Pay your partner several such compliments each day. Your efforts will reinforce the positive interactions you have with your spouse and downplay the negative ones. As American author Florence Scovel Shinn wisely wrote, "We cannot always control our thoughts, but we can control our words, and repetition impresses the subconscious."

3 exercises to help you incorporate today's theme

❶ Positively reinforce your partner's best qualities instead of pointing out her faults.

❷ Without acting on the urge, count the number of times in a day you want to criticize your partner for his or her faults. Consider what percent of these urges are reasonable, unfair, or even mean-spirited.

❸ Ask your partner how he or she copes with your faults. Listen to the answer without commenting in response.

Day 27

GOD WANTS YOU TO:
Serve Others Together

"Each one should use whatever gift he has
received to serve others, faithfully administering
God's grace in its various forms."

1 Peter 4:10

Count your blessings

Too often couples allow petty disagreements, domestic responsibilities, and work-related stressors to consume their marriage. They forget to pay attention to the good stuff, and as a result miss many chances to feel blessed. People who do not notice the bounty that surrounds them may even feel cheated. They blame God for ignoring them and turn a blind eye to those who are less fortunate. They eventually acquire a sense of entitlement that drives them to serve only themselves. Such couples are unhappy in their marriages because they have forgotten how to be grateful. But you can save your marriage—and yourself—from despair simply by serving others.

Deuteronomy 16:10 commands, "Celebrate...the Lord your God by giving a freewill offering in proportion to the blessings the Lord your God has given you." In order to give in proportion to your blessings, you must first recognize what they are. Express gratitude for every wonderful person, thing, and opportunity that crosses your path, and make special note of ways in which your partner contributes to your overall happiness. Share your recognition of these blessings with your spouse and suggest that you give back through community service as a team.

Choose a cause that is close to your heart

Most people find it is easier to serve others when they care deeply about a particular issue. Discuss various causes and charitable organizations with your spouse. Choose to serve one that calls to both of you in some way. Create a set of criteria to help you with your search. Use the following questions as a guide:

- What do we hope to accomplish?
    - o Raise money
    - o Raise awareness
    - o Teach our children about charity
- What social issues concern us the most?
    - o Homelessness
    - o Diseases such as cancer, autism, or diabetes
    - o Children in poverty
    - o The environment
    - o Animal rights
    - o Other: _____
- What are we prepared to do?
    - o Donate money
    - o Walk/run for a cause
    - o Adopt a pet or take in a foster child
    - o Volunteer time

YOUR DAILY | Act of Love

Make time today to express gratitude to God that all
of your basic needs are met. Use this as a stepping
stone to helping others meet their needs. Talk to your
partner about organizing a food drive through your
church. Share ideas for how to maximize your efforts
at your next Bible study. Use this experience to foster
camaraderie in your community and to work
as a team with your partner.

DATE ACCOMPLISHED: ....

DAILY REFLECTIONS: Write down ideas for ways you and
your partner can serve others. Include suggestions for where
you might donate money, volunteer your time, and collect
necessities for the underprivileged.

....

....

....

....

....

....

....

....

ADDITIONAL WAYS
to improve your marriage

Talk to your spouse about sponsoring a child or family in another country. This is a low-commitment method of service that requires a small monthly donation. For as little as $30 a month, reputable organizations such as World Vision and Save the Children provide clean water, nutritious meals, clothing, shelter, education, and medical care to kids and families that live in impoverished communities around the world. You can select the location, gender, and age of the child you sponsor or the family size. In exchange your family will receive regular letters, photos, and updates on the progress of your adoptee.

3 exercises to help you incorporate today's theme

❶ Volunteer to organize a toy or food drive at your workplace at a time of year other than the holidays. Since the charitable spirit is infectious this time of year, many charities are overloaded with donations in December and then starved for supplies the rest of the year. Choose a random month in the spring or summer to organize a drive for the needy.

❷ Sign up to walk for a cure with your partner—and do fundraising activities together to meet your team's financial goal. Some walks take place over the course of several days and can be turned into a memorable and meaningful trip for you and your spouse.

❸ Donate a percentage of your combined annual income to charity.

Day 28

GOD WANTS YOU TO:
Give More Than You Think You Can

"Remember this: Whoever sows sparingly will also reap sparingly, and whoever sows generously will also reap generously. Each man should give what he has decided in his heart to give, not reluctantly or under compulsion, for God loves a cheerful giver."

2 Corinthians 9:6-7

Exceed the expectations of others

Oftentimes, the effort we put forth is determined by the expectations of others. For example, if your spouse expects that you will always forget something on the grocery list, chances are that you will. Break free of disappointing performances by consistently doing more than is asked of you. Matthew 5:41 offers the following encouragement, "If someone forces you to go one mile, go with him two miles." For example, dazzle your spouse with a mouth-watering new recipe when he expects microwaveable frozen dinners on your night to cook.

Hold yourself to a higher standard

Do not be satisfied to simply eke by in life—not even when those around you do only what is required to get by. If you follow the example set by unmotivated peers, you will never grow as a person, mature as a partner, nor fulfill God's expectations of you. It is inexcusable to be mediocre when you have the potential to be exceptional—especially when it comes to your marriage. Hold yourself to a higher standard than anyone else, and you will always accomplish more than you thought possible. When you consistently do more than is expected, you raise the bar for those around you, too.

Make it your goal to inject energy back into your relationship. For as Mark Twain once wrote, "What is a man without energy? Nothing—nothing at all." Indeed, a marriage without energy does not inspire either partner to go the extra mile. Motivate yourself to go above and beyond by trying the following:

- Recall the early days of your relationship when it was your mission to impress your partner.
- Call him at work to say, "I'm thinking about you."
- Leave her favorite kind of chocolate on her pillow.
- Put all significant anniversaries and events on your calendar so you never miss one again.
- Stay up late together.
- Go to bed early together.
- Travel together.
- Dress up as if it was your first date.
- Learn a new skill and share it with your spouse.
- Plan a surprise weekend getaway.
- Download new music to his or her iPod.

YOUR DAILY | Act of Love

Tomorrow morning, get up an hour earlier than your partner. Use this time to prepare breakfast for the family, make lunch for the kids, tidy the house, and do something special for your spouse. Be creative and make it your goal to brighten his or her day. Plan ahead so you can do something truly memorable for your loved one.

DATE ACCOMPLISHED: ....

DAILY REFLECTIONS: Write about how you feel when you know your partner puts minimal effort into your relationship. In what ways does your spouse follow your lead? Do you often go the extra mile?

....

....

....

....

....

....

....

....

ADDITIONAL WAYS
to improve your marriage

As you endeavor to break through the low expectations your partner has come to set for you, do the same for him or her. Give her the benefit of the doubt in areas you have come to have rigid expectations or disappointments. For example, if your husband tends to leave his clothes around the house, don't preempt the behavior by saying something like, "Well, I'm sure you're going to leave the house a mess anyway." Give him the chance to improve upon his habits the same way you now seek to improve upon yours.

Also, remember that while you should always push your own limits, a healthy marriage requires that couples honor each other's boundaries. Identify your spouse's limits and do not cross them. For example, if your partner is a private person, do not discuss personal matters in public settings. In addition, do not try to force your spouse to give more than she is willing—with her time, money, body, emotions, etc.—but rather lead by example. As philosopher Albert Schweitzer once said, "Example is not the main thing in influencing others, it is the only thing."

3 exercises to help you incorporate today's theme

❶ Look for 2 things you can do around the house without being asked.

❷ Run an errand for your spouse you know she has been avoiding.

❸ Find one way to work hard so your partner does not have to.

Day 29

GOD WANTS YOU TO:
Develop a Positive Outlook

"If you have faith and do not doubt... If you believe,
you will receive whatever you ask for in prayer."

Matthew 21:21-22

Stop negative self-talk

It is impossible to have a positive outlook when you
constantly use negative self-talk to criticize yourself. Though
it may seem like it encourages you to do better, the opposite
is true. Thoughts that condemn your actions, intelligence,
or abilities negatively affect your attitude and limit your
successes. They also train your brain to expect the worst and
cause you to believe you will fail. Such a pessimistic attitude
has negative consequences for your marriage.

Positive self-talk, on the other hand, allows you to develop an
optimistic outlook. Optimism lets you believe that anything

is possible—including the ability to have a fulfilling marriage. Dr. Martin Seligman, director of the University of Pennsylvania Positive Psychology Center, discovered in his research that optimism offers the following benefits:

- Improved health
- Better performance
- Greater achievement
- Endurance
- Decreased instances of depression
- Less stress and longer life

Recognize when you do not have control
Dissatisfaction is inevitable when you try to control people and circumstances that are beyond your command. Likewise, when you consistently set expectations that are unattainable, you become chronically discouraged. Prolonged episodes of dissatisfaction and discouragement will eventually cause you to develop a cynical outlook. Reverse this negative spiral and improve your outlook by relinquishing control to God. Romans 15:13 offers the following encouragement, "May the God of hope fill you with all joy and peace as you trust in him." Trust that God has a plan for you, and limit your efforts to that which you can control.

Surround yourself with positive people
Unfortunately, people tend to bond over their shared complaints instead of areas in which they are content. It is easy to be negative, but it drags everyone down. Evaluate the people in your life, and decide whether they are generally positive or negative. Weed out those who are relentlessly pessimistic, and surround yourself with friends who encourage progress.

YOUR DAILY | Act of Love

Today, use positive affirmations to improve your mood—and your marriage. Write the following statements on Post-its: "I am lucky to be married to my best friend." "My marriage is successful and fulfilling." "I am deeply in love with my spouse." Then, post them in highly visible places, such as on the bathroom mirror and your dashboard.

DATE ACCOMPLISHED: ....

DAILY REFLECTIONS: Write about the ways in which your thoughts negative thoughts create a negative reality. How do your thoughts influence your marriage? Do you believe your relationship is doomed to fail or destined to succeed?

....

....

....

....

....

....

....

....

ADDITIONAL WAYS
to improve your marriage

Avoid the temptation to focus on everything that is wrong in your marriage all the time. You give far too much attention to problems when you constantly think and talk about them. As a result, issues get blown out of proportion, and you perpetuate the negativity that you claim to hate. Redirect that energy to focus on the best parts of your relationship. Dedicate ample time to what you and your partner do best together. For example, highlight your strengths as a couple by shining the spotlight on your communication skills, sex life, or ability to make each other laugh.

In this vein, limit the amount of complaining you do to your friends about your spouse. It is natural to vent or share the common challenges of relationships. But if you find yourself consistently trashing your spouse to your friends or making deprecating side comments about him or her, know that you've taken your frustrations too far. In this case, the only person you should be sharing your feelings with is your spouse.

3 exercises to help you incorporate today's theme

❶ Recite the following: "My attitude affects my marriage."

❷ Smile at your spouse even when you are in a bad mood, and think, "I am blessed!"

❸ Send an email to your spouse every morning that details one thing you are grateful for in your marriage.

Day 30

GOD WANTS YOU TO:
Banish Jealous Thoughts
from Your Mind

"Ephraim's jealousy will vanish… Ephraim
will not be jealous of Judah, nor Judah
hostile toward Ephraim."

Isaiah 11:13

Put a stop to irrational thoughts and behaviors

Jealousy is among the most dangerous feelings a person can introduce into their marriage. It feeds off of insecurity, fear, and the desire to control that which cannot be controlled. Distrust for your partner is fueled by illogical thoughts that ultimately lead to irrational behaviors. You must put an end to obsessive and unreasonable thoughts and actions if you are to gain control over jealousy and improve your relationship. Immediately disregard thoughts that cause you to mistrust your spouse. These include:

• I don't believe it when my partner says, "I love you."

- I think my spouse is having an affair.
- I suspect my partner is attracted to a co-worker.
- I can tell my spouse is unfaithful by the way he or she looks at others.
- I bet my partner fantasizes about other people.

If you engage in any of the following behaviors, stop immediately. They are a violation of your partner's privacy and trust and will only damage your relationship.

- I check my partner's Internet search history.
- I installed computer software that tracks my partner's keystrokes without his knowledge.
- I read her private emails.
- I sometimes read my spouse's journal.
- I follow my partner without her knowledge.
- I check up on my spouse with his friends and coworkers.
- I hit "redial" on my partner's cell phone to see who she called.
- I read text messages stored on my spouse's phone.
- I check my partner's pockets, purse, and wallet for clues.
- I inspect my spouse's clothes for cologne, lipstick, etc.

Improve your self image

Insecurity accounts for nearly 100 percent of all jealous thoughts. Think about it. If you were confident that you were a lovable, attractive, interesting, intelligent, and sexy partner, you would have no reason to doubt your spouse's faithfulness. The problem is not your spouse's credibility, but your self image. Boost your self-confidence and learn to like yourself, and jealous feelings will no longer control your life.

YOUR DAILY | Act of Love

Use self-talk and visual reminders to calm fears that your partner will cheat on or leave you. Write the following statement on an index card: "My partner loves and chooses me. I trust my spouse." Carry it in your purse or pocket and pull it out whenever you feel insecure about your partner's intentions.

DATE ACCOMPLISHED: ....

DAILY REFLECTIONS: Write about the reasons you are jealous. Beneath each reason include a relevant list of fears. Decide which fears must be worked through and cross the others off the list.

....
....
....
....
....
....
....
....

ADDITIONAL WAYS
to improve your marriage

If your partner is the jealous one, work to reassure him you are a faithful and trustworthy partner. First, get to the bottom of why your spouse is jealous. Have you given her reason not to trust you? Has your partner been cheated on by a previous partner? Is your spouse going through a tough time at work, or in another area of life that might cause him to be unusually insecure? Take all of this information into consideration when you react to your spouse's jealousy flare-ups. Be mindful of behaviors that make your partner uncomfortable, and never encourage your spouse's jealous tendencies just to get a reaction.

Realize, though, that you cannot get your partner to trust you simply by bending to his or her will. For example, if your partner wants to read your journal for "proof" you are not having illicit thoughts, decline to share it. Let him or her know that reading your journal is not going to make him trust you—this deep, complex emotion must come from inside him and what he believes to be true about your character and track record, and also what he believes about himself.

3 exercises to help you incorporate today's theme

❶ Talk to a minister or a close family member who will remind you that your partner is trustworthy.

❷ Look at your wedding pictures whenever you doubt your spouse's loyalty.

❸ Seek therapy if you are unable to control jealous feelings.

Day 31

GOD WANTS YOU TO:
Remain Faithful to Your Partner

"You shall not commit adultery."
Exodus 20:14

Become aware of your partner

Couples become at risk for infidelity when they stop paying attention to each other. For example, in recent years, your husband might have become a fixture on the couch that you barely notice, or your wife may move invisibly through the house, like a ghost. Even though romance, attraction, and chemistry are routinely veiled by domestic drudgery in all relationships, the vital, sexual person you married is still there beneath it.

When you ignore your partner you grow apart, and this invites temptation to sneak into your life. The desire to notice and be noticed is sometimes so powerful it causes people to have poor judgment. As a result, you might attempt to connect emotionally or even sexually with someone other than your spouse. Fight this unholy temptation and direct any lustful urges toward your spouse. Otherwise, you will offend your marriage in the eyes of God.

Improve your sex life

You may be surprised to learn that sex is not the reason most people cite for having an affair—emotional distance is. Yet couples who report greater satisfaction with their sex lives also tend to feel more deeply connected to their spouses. The attachment they feel inspires them to work to stay interested in each other and thus, they are not tempted to cheat. Tom W. Smith, author of a 2004 study of American sexual behavior, learned that most married couples only have sex about 66 times a year. Smith found that couples who reported more frequent sex with their partners rated their marriages as "happy" more often than those who rarely had sex.

Give your marriage an emotional check-up

The primary reason most people have affairs is because they feel emotionally neglected by their spouse. Do you feel overlooked by your partner? Or, perhaps you are the one who neglects your spouse. Either way, check in with your partner to discuss the status of your marriage. Ask your spouse the following questions to evaluate the emotional health of your relationship:

- Do I validate your feelings?
- Are you happy?
- What can I do to get closer to you?
- Am I a good listener?
- Do you feel that I support you?

YOUR DAILY | Act of Love

Stir up the sexual energy between you and your spouse by offering to pamper your partner in the bath or give him a massage. Create a relaxing atmosphere with soft music and lavender-scented candles. Fill the tub with warm water and bubble bath or buy luxurious new sheets for your bed. Ask your spouse to relax while you massage and pamper him or her from head to toe.

DATE ACCOMPLISHED: ....

DAILY REFLECTIONS: Write a few sentences that explore whether you encourage flirtatious relationships with anyone besides your partner. Question your motives for doing so, and imagine how you would feel if your partner did that to you.

....
....
....
....
....
....
....
....

ADDITIONAL WAYS
to improve your marriage

Matthew 5:28 warns, "Anyone who looks at a woman lustfully has already committed adultery with her in his heart." It is true that one needn't be physically intimate with someone to trespass into unfaithful waters. Flirting with people who are not your spouse truly constitutes flirting with disaster.

Make it a point to avoid engaging in any suggestive, flirtatious, or otherwise inappropriate behavior with people who are not your spouse. This includes deleting the phone numbers and emails of all ex-boyfriends and girlfriends, refraining from engaging in a "harmless" flirtation with someone at work, and avoiding "single girl or guy" behavior when out with your friends. It is easy to check whether your behavior falls under the category of inappropriate. Picture your spouse sitting next to you as you talk to your coworker, watching you dance while out with your friends, or reading the Facebook messages you trade with an ex. If your spouse would approve, the behavior is something you can be proud of, too.

3 exercises to help you incorporate today's theme

❶ Pray for the strength to stick to your vows.

❷ Surprise your partner with an overnight stay in a nice hotel room.

❸ Chant, "I choose to be a faithful and loyal partner" until the temptation to stray subsides.

Day 32

GOD WANTS YOU TO:
Be Nonjudgemental
With Your Partner

"'Do not judge and you will not be judged. Do not
condemn, and you will not be condemned.'"

Luke 6:37

Leave judgment to God

There are many responsibilities that God passes on to
married couples. He requires them to love, honor, and obey
each other. It is written in His law to be faithful and kind.
God does not, however, ask you to pass judgment. This is
a role He reserves for Himself. In Exodus 6:6, for example,
God declares, "I will redeem you with an outstretched arm
and with mighty acts of judgment."

Focus on your own growth

People who constantly assess the value of others' thoughts
and actions often ignore their own shortcomings. One way,
therefore, to overcome these judgmental tendencies is to turn
your focus inward. However, do not cease judging others
only to judge yourself. Rather, nurture your own growth
as an individual and as a partner to your spouse. Evaluate

areas of your life in which you could do a better job. Set goals for improvement, and come up with a course of action to meet them. Use the following model to help you create your own growth plan:

Shortcoming: I often judge my partner harshly when she makes a mistake.

Goal: To stop being judgmental of others, especially my spouse.

Plan of Action: Instead of pointing out my partner's flaws and errors, I will do the following:

- Be silent until the urge to judge passes.
- Keep my facial expressions neutral.
- Promise to let my partner make mistakes.
- Admit I am flawed and in no position to judge.
- Consider that my partner's way of doing things works for him or makes her happy.

Keep it to yourself

It may seem impossible to kick your judgmental habit. You might even feel as though the tendency to pass judgment is too tightly wound into your personality to be extricated, or that the only way to stop is to completely change who you are. This may be true, but one step you can immediately take is to keep judgments to yourself. Though it is undesirable to have judgmental thoughts about others, it becomes harmful when you express them. Bite your lip, cover your mouth, or take a vow of silence. Then allow any judgmental thoughts to come and go from your mind without giving voice to them.

YOUR DAILY | Act of Love

Today, refrain from making judgmental statements
to your spouse, such as, "If I had been in charge…"
or "What a ridiculous thing to say!" Comments like
these are insulting and hurtful. Remember that you are
equals, and treat your partner with respect. Indeed,
as Ralph Waldo Emerson wisely wrote, "Men are
respectable only as they respect."

DATE ACCOMPLISHED: ....

DAILY REFLECTIONS: Write down what qualifies you
to pass judgment on your partner's behavior, decisions, or
opinions. Do you think you are better than your spouse? Are
you the moral compass for your relationship?

....

....

....

....

....

....

....

....

ADDITIONAL WAYS
to improve your marriage

If you are a judgmental person, you probably don't have as many friends as you used to. Associate U.S. Supreme Court Justice Abe Fortas once pointed out that passing judgment was a lonely profession. He said, "Judging is a lonely job in which a man is, as near as may be, an island entire." Since you are not a Supreme Court justice, you have no responsibility to generate or share judgmental thoughts with others. Interrupt them with a loud clap by thinking, "STOP!" to yourself whenever you feel the urge to judge come over you. Shake your head vigorously; replace the thought with a positive observation about the person. Do whatever it takes to break up your thoughts so that your holier-than-thou attitude does not leave you completely alone.

3 exercises to help you incorporate today's theme

❶ Allow your partner to do things his way, regardless of how frustrating it is for you.

❷ Never judge your spouse to your children. Statements like, "Mommy was naughty and spent too much money" or "Daddy is so bad at this, it's no wonder it didn't get done right" are manipulative and unfair.

❸ Express disappointment in your spouse's behavior, but learn to do so without attacking his or her character.

Day 33

GOD WANTS YOU TO:
Learn to Be Quiet Together

"When Boaz had finished eating and drinking and
was in good spirits, he went over to lie down at the
far end of the grain pile. Ruth approached quietly,
uncovered his feet and lay down."

Ruth 3:7

Use nonverbal communication to express yourself
Think of how close you feel to your spouse when you hold
each other, dance, and have sex. All of these activities are
action-oriented and require close, physical contact. Indeed,
the deepest bonds with your partner are formed by what
you do together, not by what you say. As an experiment,
seek to enhance intimacy in your marriage by using body
language to communicate instead of words.

Develop your ability to connect with your spouse without
words. If quiet expression does not come naturally to you,
try one of the following:

- Connect with your partner in public:
    - o Make eye contact from across the room.
    - o Tilt your head and smile.
    - o Wave your hand.
    - o Touch his or her shoulder.
    - o Wink.
    - o Blow a kiss.
    - o Raise your eyebrows.
- Connect with your partner in private:
    - o Place your hand on the small of her back.
    - o Put your head on his shoulder.
    - o Hold hands.
    - o Kiss her neck.
    - o Smile when he looks at you.

Talk less

Couples are encouraged to talk about everything, from feelings to finances. But sometimes the quickest way to your partner's heart is to be quiet. For a couple of hours, let 99 percent of what is on your mind go without verbally expressing it. Sift through your thoughts to weed out all but the most important issues and urgent business matters. The reward of your efforts will be well worth the work. As British philosopher Bertrand Russell noted, "A happy life must be to a great extent a quiet life, for it is only in an atmosphere of quiet that true joy dare live."

Give your spouse room to be quiet

How many times have you thought, "I would give anything to have a quiet evening to myself!" If you thought it, chances are your partner has too. Give your spouse one quiet night alone in the house. Use this time to hit the gym or see a movie with friends.

YOUR DAILY | Act of Love

Tonight, plan to spend a quiet evening with your spouse. Turn off the television, and put all PDAs, cell phones, and laptops in another room. If you have children, arrange for them to spend the night at grandma's house or with a friend. Challenge your partner to a game of chess or work on a crossword puzzle together. Talk as little as possible, and enjoy the comfortable silence shared by longtime companions.

DATE ACCOMPLISHED: ....

DAILY REFLECTIONS: For one hour, write down your thoughts instead of saying them out loud to your partner. Once they are on paper, evaluate them. What thoughts were probably unnecessary to share? What thoughts were you sharing only to have something to say?

....

....

....

....

....

....

....

....

ADDITIONAL WAYS
to improve your marriage

Help your marriage by coming to terms with why you might be averse to quiet time. Does silence make you uncomfortable? Do you interpret periods of silence as a sign that something is wrong? Do you worry that having nothing to talk about means that you and your partner are bored with each other? All of these are reasonable fears but still do not constitute good reasons for talking just to say something.

Realize that being quiet with your partner does not necessarily indicate a problem in your relationship. In fact, talking just for the sake of talking reflects a discomfort that is often far more serious than silence. Understand that life with your partner is long—surely the whole of your relationship cannot be dominated by conversation. By learning to appreciate quiet time with your partner, you learn to experience and love a whole new side of your relationship.

3 exercises to help you incorporate today's theme

❶ Split up the newspaper on Sunday mornings and read it together over breakfast.

❷ Schedule a couple's massage.

❸ Spend quiet time in nature. Go for a hike, rent a canoe, or take a walk through a part of town to which you have never been.

Day 34

GOD WANTS YOU TO:
Share Your Time
Without Complaint

"Do everything without complaining or arguing,
so that you may become blameless and pure."
Philippians 2:14-15

Make the best out of the worst

In a perfect world, everyone in your family would enjoy doing the same things. In reality, however, you must sometimes participate in unpleasant activities, attend boring events, and have discussions with people whom you do not like. Indeed, the responsibilities of having a family require that you compromise for the good of the group. There are two ways to deal with the less-fun aspects of family life: you can complain about it, or you can make the best out of the worst.

Find something to be positive about in every situation. Avoid a syrupy-sweet, greeting card positivity, though, because it will not read as genuine. Just find one small thing to applaud. For example, if your partner needs surgery, point out how nice the nurse is or that you were lucky get a private hospital room. Norman Vincent Peale, author of *The Power of Positive Thinking*, put it best when he said, "Any fact facing us is not as important as our attitude toward it, for that determines our success or failure."

Give your time freely

The demands of marriage and parenthood can be overwhelming. It is exhausting to expend so much energy on others—sometimes with little to no recognition for your efforts. But as Abraham Lincoln wisely said, "Don't worry when you are not recognized, but strive to be worthy of recognition." Indeed, be generous with your time, effort, love, and affection. Do not expect to be thanked for picking your children up at school, nor rewarded for attending your partner's holiday party for work. Remember that time is the most precious commodity you have to share with your loved ones. Give it freely—and without complaint.

Make the positive choice

Denis Waitley, author of *The Psychology of Winning*, once wrote, "There are two primary choices in life: to accept conditions as they exist, or accept the responsibility for changing them." Indeed, time spent complaining is time wasted. What if you chose not to complain about chores, errands, or having to spend quality time with your spouse? Complaining essentially guarantees a miserable experience. On the other hand, people who predict a great outcome make decisions along the way that yield the best possible results.

YOUR DAILY | Act of Love

Today, spend time arranging your work schedule so that you are able to make it home in time for dinner at least 3 times this week. On these nights, help your partner prepare the meal and set the table. Round up the kids, turn off the television, and sit down together at the dining room table. Lead everyone in prayer, and express your gratitude to God for your family.

DATE ACCOMPLISHED: ....

DAILY REFLECTIONS: Write about why you protest when your partner asks you to spend more time with your family. What would you rather be doing? How can you make this time more enjoyable?

....
....
....
....
....
....
....
....

ADDITIONAL WAYS
to improve your marriage

Let Romans 12:10 inspire you to share your time without complaint. As it instructs: "Be devoted to one another in brotherly love. Honor one another above yourselves." One way to honor your spouse above yourself is take the initiative with housework. Sure, you may hate to clean the bathroom, but do you think your partner looks forward to cleaning toilets any more than you do? It is unlikely, so don't treat your partner like a housekeeper.

With this in mind, participate in domestic chores without having to be asked and don't complain while doing them. Live up to the partnership that is your marriage by taking equal responsibility in getting the unpleasant or daunting work done. Chances are your spouse will be grateful for the help—and for being able to shed his or her role as a nag.

3 exercises to help you incorporate today's theme

❶ Keep your partner company while he runs errands.

❷ Attend a social event at the request of your spouse at least twice a month.

❸ Take your children to visit an elderly relative once a month.

Day 35

GOD WANTS YOU TO:
Be Content Without Becoming Complacent

"I have learned the secret of being content in any and every situation, whether well fed or hungry, whether living in plenty or in want. I can do everything through him who gives me strength."
Philippians 4:12-13

Look good for your spouse

When a person becomes complacent, they get lazy, and laziness leads to unattractiveness. In fact, a major complaint of long-term married couples is that their spouses stopped caring about their appearances after a certain point. The disappointment they express usually applies to weight gain, style of dress, hygiene, and general health. When one partner stops taking care of himself or herself, their spouse often takes it as a sign that the romance is over.

If you want your spouse to continue to be attracted to you, take as much care with your appearance as you used to. Consult the following list of appearance "do's" and "don'ts" to get your partner to take a second look:

- Do exercise at least 3 to 5 times a week.
- Do bathe every day.
- Do follow food guidelines laid out by the U.S. Department of Health and Human Services (www.health.gov/DietaryGuidelines/dga2005/document/default.htm)
- Do dress up for your partner.
- Do get your hair cut and styled.
- Do wear clothing that flatters your body type.
- Do go to bed naked.

- Don't avoid physical activity.
- Don't eat junk food, take-out, or drink too much alcohol.
- Don't wear the same outfit every day.
- Don't neglect your hair and nails.
- Don't wear ripped, baggy, or too-small clothing.
- Don't wear old, bulky T-shirts to bed.

Deal with boredom

Boredom can be a temporary phase or a signal that your marriage needs work. Fortunately, inventiveness and a can-do attitude can bring your relationship back to life. Liven up your marriage by being a couple first. Too often, we put our career and children before the relationship with our spouse. Put energy back into your partnership and let everything else come second. Also, work to maintain your edge. We all lose part of our identity to some extent when we get married. Women take their husband's name, and men answer to their wives. Work to preserve your most unique qualities and do not compromise your individuality.

YOUR DAILY | Act of Love

Surprise your partner today with a new look. Get a makeover without mentioning it beforehand. Do something completely different with your hair—cut it short, change the color, get highlights, or wear a smart hat. Dress contrary to your normal look, and accessorize with a new scent. Purchase new, sexy underwear to complete your look and top off the surprise.

DATE ACCOMPLISHED: ....

DAILY REFLECTIONS: It is normal to experience bouts of boredom in your marriage. Write a few lines about why you think they occur and what you might do to shake up your relationship. Note how your attitude and energy affect the periods of boredom you and your spouse experience.

....

....

....

....

....

....

....

....

ADDITIONAL WAYS
to improve your marriage

Of the 65 percent of adults in the U.S. who are overweight or obese, a significant number are married. The fact is that many couples get fat and lazy when they are complacent. A busy lifestyle, a pantry stocked with sugary snacks, and little time to exercise leads to poor food choices and an unhealthy weight. The problem worsens when one partner enables the other's sedentary lifestyle, or when both stop caring about what the other thinks of them.

You can rescue your relationship from both the physical and emotional health risks of obesity. Try cooking healthy meals at home more often and get out for walks with your spouse a few nights a week. It will improve your health—and your marriage. In addition to thinking about how God wants you to respect the body He gave you, consider that the better care you and your spouse take of each other, the more likely it is you will live a long, fulfilling life together.

3 exercises to help you incorporate today's theme

❶ Sit down together and decide on a menu for the week; then shop for and cook the meals together!

❷ Sign up for weekly ballroom dance lessons with your spouse.

❸ Train together to meet a physical challenge, such as hiking a difficult trail or running a half-marathon.

Day 36

GOD WANTS YOU TO:
Avoid Coveting Others' Lifestyles

"You...covet, but you cannot have what you want.
You quarrel and fight. You do not have, because
you do not ask God."

James 4:2

Seek satisfaction in what is around you

The man who wakes up every day and focuses on what he
lacks feels poor, lonely, and dissatisfied. He looks around
at his friends, neighbors, even strangers, and thinks, "They
don't know how good they have it!" He feels jealous and
angry toward celebrities for their wealth and success. His
discontent grows daily to accommodate all the things he
covets: wealth, status, power, respect, possessions, good
looks, and relationships. He is so busy categorizing what
others have that he completely ignores his own bounty.

God warned against such ignorance in Exodus 20:17: "You
shall not covet your neighbor's house. You shall not covet
your neighbor's wife...or anything that belongs to your
neighbor." Indeed, the quickest route to a miserable life is to
covet others' lifestyles.

On the other hand, appreciating what you have ensures a happy existence. Seek satisfaction in what is around you by first acknowledging that life itself is a gift. Show God that you cherish your existence by:

- Practicing good health.
- Nurturing your spirituality.
- Making ethical decisions.
- Banishing jealous, covetous thoughts.
- Treating everyone (including yourself) with compassion.

Honor and cherish the life you have built with your spouse

Consider that when you covet the lifestyle of others you diminish the value of your way of life. This can be hard for your spouse to take and will hurt your relationship. From this point on, reserve compliments and positive observations for your own life with your spouse. Your positivity and enthusiasm will create opportunities for growth, whereas a negative attitude will inhibit them. Appreciate the blessings in your life, which are surely many, and it will pave the way for more good. As Oprah Winfrey said, "Be thankful for what you have; you'll end up having more. If you concentrate on what you don't have, you will never, ever have enough."

Realize that the grass isn't always greener

Every seemingly perfect life has its flaws. Rich, beautiful, and powerful people all falter, fail, and experience pain. Do not delude yourself into thinking that you "would just be happy if...." Having someone else's circumstance wouldn't fix your marital issues. Only you can. And remember, the lives you covet all have their own problems and pains, despite a pristine exterior.

YOUR DAILY | Act of Love

Take time today to write a letter to God thanking Him for the elements of your marriage that you like best. Be detailed in your description of what brings you joy in your relationship. Make special note of qualities unique to your spouse. Use only positive language, avoid comparisons, and be effusive in your communication with God. Share the final version with your partner.

DATE ACCOMPLISHED: ....

DAILY REFLECTIONS: Write a few sentences about how more money or a bigger house would improve your relationship. Make sure to also consider the problems in your life that such an influx would not fix. Finally, ask yourself: If you are not grateful now, what makes you think you will be satisfied with more?

....

....

....

....

....

....

....

....

ADDITIONAL WAYS
to improve your marriage

A surefire way to put a stop to covetous thoughts is to make your marriage one to envy. To this end, nurture the relationship you have with your spouse on every level. Practice effective communication skills to limit misunderstandings and to increase emotional closeness. Enhance your spiritual connection when you pray together and attend regular church services. Liven up your sex life with toys and role play. Devote time to laugh and play together in support of your friendship. Present a united front in everything you do and eventually, you will feel like the team you were when your relationship began.

3 exercises to help you incorporate today's theme

❶ Draw a tree on a large sheet of paper. Use vibrant colors to fill in the leaves, and on each one write something special about your family, church, or job.

❷ Keep an updated family scrapbook. Include a brief description of fond memories with photos from all significant milestones.

❸ Set goals and work with your partner to achieve them. For example, contribute a percentage of your monthly income toward a dream vacation in Europe.

Day 37

GOD WANTS YOU TO:
Never Raise Your Hands in Anger

"I want men everywhere to lift up holy hands in
prayer, without anger or disputing."
1 Timothy 2:8

Nothing justifies violence against your partner
The Centers for Disease Control states that 1 in 4 women
will become a victim of domestic violence in her lifetime. Of
the women who are abused, 85 percent of them are assaulted
by a boyfriend or husband. Interestingly, men are victims of
abuse too, though the numbers are lower and most cases of
abuse go unreported.

Of course, you cannot help becoming annoyed with your
partner now and then. In turn, you might argue, fight, yell,
or storm out of your house in a fit of rage. But there is a line
you must never cross—regardless of how angry you feel or
how serious the nature of your partner's provocation. There
is never any excuse for using your hands as a weapon, and

you must never hit, push, or otherwise physically threaten your spouse. Look to Isaiah 54:9 for inspiration whenever the urge to be violent rises up. It reads, "I have sworn not to be angry with you, never to rebuke you again."

Do not use your hands to intimidate your spouse

Your hands are capable of conveying great love through touch and gestures. But they can also become powerful weapons. Understand that you never have permission to raise your hands in anger. Likewise, it is unacceptable to throw objects at your spouse or to make your partner flinch into submission. Not only is violence wrong, it rarely accomplishes anything productive. As author Isaac Asimov wisely wrote, "Violence is the last refuge of the incompetent." Seek other, nonviolent ways to resolve conflicts within your marriage, such as couples counseling.

Teach your children to be nonviolent

Peace activist Colman McCarthy once warned, "Unless we teach our children peace, somebody else will teach them violence." Create a home that is a sanctuary free of violent television shows, movies, and video games. Have frequent, open discussions with your kids about any violent influences in their lives. Teach your children how to reach peaceful solutions, and practice nonviolence—in all its forms—by practicing it at home. Model loving-kindness, compassion, and non-threatening conflict resolution in every interaction you have with your spouse. Lastly, provide your children with the reasoning skills to be able to fight using their words instead of their hands.

YOUR DAILY | Act of Love

Use your hands to touch your partner whenever possible. Touch her hair, rub his back, and focus on allowing loving energy to flow from your hands to your spouse. When you are angry, stretch your hands open and spread your fingers apart instead of clenching them into fists. Think, "My hands are instruments of gentle affection" until the urge to raise them passes.

DATE ACCOMPLISHED: ....

DAILY REFLECTIONS: Write about how you feel when you become angry. Take note of all physical symptoms and thoughts that cross through your head. Ask yourself if getting physically angry ever actually solved a problem in the long-term.

....

....

....

....

....

....

....

....

ADDITIONAL WAYS
to improve your marriage

People who constantly feel under financial and job-related pressures reside in an emotional anger-zone. Because they are wound so tightly, they rarely think before they react. This level of tension is unhealthy and may lead to regrettable actions. If you feel chronically stressed, routinely angry, or unbearably frustrated, start attending a yoga class. Yoga gives you the tools to control your physical responses to stress and anger. It links your body and mind so they operate as one—which allows you greater control over your thoughts and actions. With regular practice, you will experience a noticeable reduction in tension, anger, and frustration—and so will those around you.

3 exercises to help you incorporate today's theme

❶ Burn off energy with exercise. Do something vigorous to release tension on a regular basis, like join a boxing gym or take a spinning class.

❷ Meditate for 15 minutes each morning and evening. Sit in a quiet room and take several deep breaths. Focus on the rhythm of your breath. Allow thoughts to enter and leave your mind without judgment.

❸ Enroll in an anger management class or seek therapy if you cannot control your temper.

Day 38

GOD WANTS YOU TO:
Speak Graciously to Your Mate

"He who loves a pure heart
and whose speech is gracious will
have the king for his friend."

Proverbs 22:11

Speak clearly and effectively

Facilitate smooth communications with your spouse by using clear, effective language to express yourself. Avoid repetition, and say what you mean with bold honesty. It can be very frustrating to have a conversation with someone who says something and then retracts it with, "Just kidding!" Likewise, limit the amount of ironic and sarcastic comments you inject into casual conversation with your spouse. Otherwise, you may become hooked on speaking in riddles instead of simply saying what you mean.

Put extra thought into what you say before you speak— and be respectful of how you say it. Be considerate of the timing when you bring up difficult topics, and be patient with your partner's responses. Always be mindful of your tone and volume when you deliver bad news, give criticism, or speak angrily to your spouse. Avoid misunderstandings by annunciating when you talk, and do not mumble or make side comments.

Know when to listen

Think and Grow Rich author Napoleon Hill once quipped, "Wise men, when in doubt whether to speak or to keep quiet, give themselves the benefit of the doubt, and remain silent." Indeed, much of the trouble that couples encounter when they try to communicate has to do with their inability to keep quiet. Learn how to remain silent when you are at risk for insulting or offending your partner with your words. Count to ten, shrug, or proclaim, "I don't know what to say," when you are tempted to speak discourteously to your spouse. Above all, listen to what your spouse has to say without using the time to think of what you will say next.

Never shush your spouse

Regardless of how you actually feel about what your spouse says in public, do not let on that you are embarrassed. Always be supportive when your partner is unable to be articulate. Do not tell him to shut up or talk over him, and definitely do not make fun of him in front of others. Do, however, provide her with the tools to save face in embarrassing situations. Use this moment to rescue her with affection and encouragement. For example, say something like, "Honey, I know how frustrating it is to get tongue-tied in front of people, but you handled yourself very well!"

YOUR DAILY | Act of Love

Use today to take a time-out from making demands.
Rather, make requests. Start by reintroducing
pleasantries into every conversation with your spouse.
For example, instead of saying, "I hate this show! Give
me the remote!" Say, "I'd like to change the channel
if you don't mind. Please hand me the clicker." Your
partner is much more likely to oblige your requests
when you ask nicely.

DATE ACCOMPLISHED: ....

DAILY REFLECTIONS: Write about the way you speak to
your partner. How is it perceived by your children? What do
you think your tone, word choice, and volume teaches your
kids about communication and respect?

....

....

....

....

....

....

....

....

ADDITIONAL WAYS
to improve your marriage

If gracious communication is not your strong suit, read the romantic classics for inspiration. Of course, you will probably never speak the way William Shakespeare wrote. But you can adopt the spirit in which the main characters in Romeo and Juliet communicated their affection for each other. Learn to use language the way Elizabeth Bennet and Mr. Darcy used their wit and charm to create a heightened level of love and sexual tension in Jane Austen's *Pride and Prejudice*. If you do not have time to read these classics, make a date to watch the film versions with your partner instead.

3 exercises to help you incorporate today's theme

❶ Refer to your spouse by affectionate nicknames.

❷ Avoid putting a sarcastic spin on terms of endearment. For example, "Thanks for nothing, babe."

❸ Speak to your partner as if God is in the room, listening.

Day 39

GOD WANTS YOU TO:
Develop an Appreciation for the Big Picture

"Do not conform any longer to the pattern of this world, but be transformed by the renewing of your mind. Then you will be able to test and approve what God's will is—his good, pleasing and perfect will."

Romans 12:2

Take the good with the bad

You may experience long stretches in which you feel emotionally unconnected to your spouse. There will be less sex and more arguments when this period descends, because you aren't seeing eye to eye. While such periods are disconcerting as they are happening, remember that every relationship has its ups and downs, its highs and lows. The way to get through the lows and downs is to be confident they are just a phase.

Couples who expect to encounter difficulties at various points in their marriages are better equipped to handle them. They have reasonable expectations of their partners and are able to quickly bounce back from disappointment. Such couples understand that a fight—even a big one—does not mean that divorce is imminent. They take comfort in their long view, because they know that their commitment is forever—and that the fight is just a temporary setback. The big picture, they realize, must have enough room to incorporate both the good and the bad.

Make decisions that support your broader view

Like most Americans, your master plan is probably to have a happy marriage, raise successful children, own a nice home, earn a decent living, and be comforted by your spiritual life. Taken together, these elements form your big picture. Thus, every decision you make should support one or more of these ideas. It will help to articulate what your goals are, and then break them down into small, achievable steps. Check off each accomplishment that brings you closer to reaching your greater goals.

Don't get hung up on the small stuff

Look at your life on a macro level to make the big picture become a real presence in your life. When it does you will develop the confidence, patience, and the perspective to weather any challenge. When you no longer put every little thing under the microscope, you will not get hung up on the trivial and fleeting. You will realize that your life has purpose, your actions have meaning, and that everything makes sense within the context of your big picture.

YOUR DAILY | Act of Love

To get a bird's eye view of your relationship, create a timeline of it. Start with the first time you met your partner and mark down every significant milestone you have shared since. Include your first kiss, any noteworthy trips or moves, your wedding day, the birthdays of your children, and other events. Allow the continuum of your relationship to continue with an ellipsis that extends past your senior years.

DATE ACCOMPLISHED: ....

DAILY REFLECTIONS: The way you react to crises, arguments, and rough patches in your relationship is very telling. Write a few sentences about how you tend to react to such events. Do you think you are a person of long- or short-term vision?

....
....
....
....
....
....
....
....

ADDITIONAL WAYS
to improve your marriage

Zero in on your big picture by visualizing your life as a novel. Imagine that it will be read by future generations of your family, and be creative and specific with the details. Outline the beginning, middle, and end of the story, and come up with one main plot or overarching theme. Identify the major characters, describe where the action takes place, and make all the details support your theme. When you get to the end of this exercise, ask yourself: "What is the moral of my story?" Your answer will reveal your big picture—and may even make a great a title for your book.

3 exercises to help you incorporate today's theme

❶ Come up with a slogan that captures your general attitude and philosophy in life.

❷ List 3 major goals you would like to accomplish with your spouse within the next 5 years. Then, list another 3 to accomplish in the 10 years after that. List a final 3 for the following 10 years. Look over what you've written. These goals constitute the skeleton of your big picture.

❸ Think of times you thought your relationship was doomed for failure, and focus on how you and your partner bounced back.

Day 40

GOD WANTS YOU TO:
Be Strong for Your Partner

"Be strong and let us fight bravely for our
people and the cities of our God."
2 Samuel 10:12

Be the one to make difficult decisions
Some people thrive under pressure, and others crumble
beneath the weight of it. It is vital to your marriage that
you thrive when your partner crumbles, and vice versa.
Otherwise, you are left with two leaders—or, worse, a
situation in which neither partner is capable of taking
action. Thus, when your partner becomes unable to make
difficult or rational decisions due to grief, fear, sickness, or
depression, you must step up and be the strong one.

Situations that arise in which you alone decide the outcome
require that you are strong in your resolve. Once you make a
hard choice, you cannot waiver, change your mind, or undo
it. Your spouse will look to you as the leader, and trust that

you know what you are doing. If you falter in that role, your spouse will second-guess your ability to lead and you will both be sent back to square one.

Share the responsibility

We are all, to some degree, held captive by our fears that others will judge us harshly or decide they do not like us. One way to prevent your spouse from having to suffer from his or her unpopular decisions is to share the responsibility of them. Even if you did not make the actual decision, stand in solidarity with your partner against those affected by his or her choices. Tell children it was "our" decision when they are disappointed with the verdict. Apologize to your mother-in-law for forgetting her birthday, even if you feel your husband should be responsible for that task. Present a united front to absorb some of the heat from those affected. And never agree with people who criticize your partner's decisions.

Make the necessary arrangements

Help your partner in times of great crisis—such as when there is a death in the family—by making all of the necessary arrangements. Offer to take on either supporting or leading role throughout the ordeal. Some examples of what you could do in that case include:

- Locate important documents
- Schedule and attend appointments
- Field phone calls from well-wishers
- Explain the situation to your children and keep them occupied

YOUR DAILY | Act of Love

Marriage should offer each partner a safety net in times of need. Today, ask yourself what you can do to prevent your partner from free-falling in response to illness, stress, or grief. Learn if your spouse is feeling overwhelmed and offer to carry the lion's share of the load for a while until your partner recovers.

DATE ACCOMPLISHED: ....

DAILY REFLECTIONS: Write down several occasions when you had to be strong for your partner. What specifically did you do, and what encouraged you to step up and rescue your spouse?

....

....

....

....

....

....

....

....

ADDITIONAL WAYS
to improve your marriage

Meeting the challenges of any problem is difficult; but when your spouse feels like he or she has no idea what to do, the distress increases and the problem seems hopeless. You can help your partner get a handle on the situation by offering up possible solutions. Take charge and present her with an either/or scenario. For example, if paying the mortgage is the problem, offer the following choices: "Either we refinance our loan or we consider bankruptcy." Sometimes there will not be a desirable answer but having choices make a person feel at least somewhat in control. As American writer Rita Mae Brown once noted, "A peacefulness follows any decision, even the wrong one."

3 exercises to help you incorporate today's theme

❶ Practice being a leader in low-risk situations or emergencies that are minor in nature. Becoming accustomed to trusting your instincts and leading others will help you fall naturally back on these qualities should a major disaster or problem emerge.

❷ Create a step-by-step plan to follow during emergencies so you are prepared to take on a leadership role.

❸ Strategize the probable outcome of all decisions. For each course of action, chart at least 3 resulting actions that are like to follow. Use these resulting actions to better assess the choices before you.

AFTER

THE 40 DAYS

WHAT HAPPENS NEXT...

At this point, you have spent 40 days completing the Daily Acts of Love and exercises for each theme—this has been quite a lot of work, no doubt. The dedication it takes to save your relationship extends far beyond these 40 days, however. It is not enough to read this book once and set it aside. Use prayer, communication, and the many themes you studied here to continue to work daily at your partnership, love, and friendship. Refer to the following chapter for additional resources to help you continue working diligently at your marriage every day.

USE THE SPACE BELOW FOR OTHER

significant thoughts, emotions, or reflections:

_____

_____

_____

_____

_____

_____

_____

_____

_____

_____

_____

_____

_____

_____

_____

_____

_____

_____

_____

Marriage Q & A

Much of your ability to fix problems within your marriage hinges on your willingness to answer the following questions: What was your relationship like in the beginning? How does the beginning of your marriage compare with its current state? And, what do you want your marriage to look like in the future? Indeed, to know where you are going, you must understand where you and your partner have come from.

Ask yourself the following questions to help you better understand your marriage:

The Beginning

1. What first attracted you to your spouse?
2. What did you do on your first date?
3. Why did you agree to a second date?
4. Who planned most of your dates?
5. How long did you date before you got engaged?
6. How long were you engaged before you were married?
7. Did you wait to have sex until after you were married?

8. What used to be your shared interests?
9. What used to be your differences?
10. How did you used to deal with conflict?

The Present

1. Do you enjoy your partner's company?
2. How often do you go out as a couple?
3. Do you look forward to dates with your spouse?
4. Who usually suggests that you go out together?
5. How many times a week do you have alone time with your partner?
6. How often do you have sex?
7. Are you satisfied with your sex life?
8. Who usually initiates sex?
9. What do you have in common with your spouse?
10. How often do you fight/argue/disagree?

The Future

1. Do you want to be married to your spouse for the rest of your life?
2. Would you be happy with your marriage if it stayed as it is now for the next 25 years?
3. In what ways do you hope your marriage stays the same?
4. In what ways do you want it to change?
5. What can you do to make your marriage more satisfying in the future?

6. What expectations do you have of your spouse for improving your relationship?
7. How important is companionship to the future of your marriage?
8. What role does God play in the betterment of your relationship with your spouse?
9. How can increasing God's presence in your home positively affect your marriage?
10. Are you willing to do anything it takes to have the best marriage possible?

Ask your spouse to answer the same questions, and compare your answers. Let yourselves engage in an honest dialogue, and don't censor your explanations. Agree to suffer together through difficult answers so that you may both be cleansed of any hurt or doubt. Make it your goal to come through this exercise united and strong.

USE THE SPACE BELOW FOR OTHER

significant thoughts, emotions, or reflections:

_____

_____

_____

_____

_____

_____

_____

_____

_____

_____

_____

_____

_____

_____

_____

_____

_____

_____

_____

Admit to Wrongdoing and Repent

It is nearly impossible to escape this life without having committed at least one transgression against your vows. However, you may be in denial about yours, especially if they occurred a long time ago. To truly fix your marriage, you must admit to and repent for these transgressions before you can move on with a clean conscience. In doing so, it is not necessary to admit every little wrongdoing to your partner— but is important to be honest with yourself. If you doubt whether you should tell your partner something you did, seek counsel from your pastor. He or she will be able to guide you toward right action and repentance.

Use the following questionnaire to lead you toward a clean conscience and an honest marriage:

1. Have you ever lied to your spouse? If so, what about?
2. Have you ever raised your hands in anger toward your partner?
3. Do you ever have sexual thoughts about people other than your spouse? Have you ever acted on them?
4. Have you ever let your partner take the blame for your actions?
5. Do you ever shut your spouse out because you feel guilty about something? If so, what do you feel guilty about?
6. Have your actions ever led to serious consequences

for your spouse? For example, an accident, arrest, financial hardship, or depression?

7. Has your spouse ever trusted you with information, only to have you betray his or her confidence?
8. Have you ever hid money from your partner?
9. Do you ever pretend to listen to your spouse talk?
10. Have you ever said something hurtful to your partner on purpose?

Repent for your actions in one or more of the following ways:

1. Tell your spouse the entire truth and issue a heartfelt apology.
2. Confess your sins to a priest or pastor and ask for forgiveness.
3. Share your wrongdoings with God and pray for His forgiveness.
4. Make it up to your partner—by returning the money, telling the truth, etc.
5. Take responsibility for your actions to all interested parties.
6. Promise never to do the same thing to your partner again—and mean it.
7. End a flirtation or affair immediately if you are unfaithful.
8. Seek professional help for an alcohol, drug, gambling, or anger problem.
9. Vow to keep your partner's confidences in the future.
10. Ask your partner what you can do to fix the situation and accept his or her answer.

Evaluate God's Presence in Your Marriage

Many books focus on fixing marital problems. But this book involves God in the process because when a couple is grounded in faith, they are more likely to rise above the challenges they face. They are more likely to have a holy and perfect union and are more likely to reflect the positive, divine qualities that make our world a better place.

Therefore, it is critical to involve God in the process of fixing your marriage. Consider the following:

1. How has your love for God inspired you to be a better partner?
2. In what ways does your marriage exemplify God's love?
3. Do you pray with your spouse? How often?
4. Are you motivated by God to keep your commitment to your spouse?
5. In what ways do you find comfort in the Word?
6. Do you consider yourself to be faithfully executing your vows?

7. How have your spiritual ties strengthened your marriage?
8. Is your spouse a faithful person?
9. Do you regularly seek answers to problems in the Bible?
10. Do you accept your partner's flaws as God accepts yours?
11. Do you have a particular Bible passage or reading that you turn to in times of need?
12. Do you have a relationship with a pastor or figure of spiritual guidance who you can contact when you have questions or are struggling?

Your Community

The company you keep says a lot about who you are and what influences you. Surround yourself with positive marital role models and you will aspire to be better at your marriage. On the contrary, if the majority of your friends are single, unhappily married, separated, or divorced, you may be tempted to give up on your relationship and fall in with the crowd.

Learn whether the company you and your partner keep supports your values by answering the following questions:

1. Where did you meet your friends? At work? Church? Did you grow up together?
2. Do you and your spouse have many happily married friends?
3. Do you and your partner tend to socialize together or individually?
4. Do you like each others' friends?
5. Does your spouse have friends who you disapprove of? If so, why?

6. Does your partner complain about your behavior (drinking, cursing, smoking, coming home late, etc.) when you go out with certain friends?

7. Do your friends share the same values as you and your partner?

8. Would you call your group of friends a community?

9. Do the people you spend time with inspire you to be a better husband or wife?

10. Are you encouraged or discouraged about the future of your marriage based on the examples set by your closest friends?

Seek Further Inspiration from the Bible

...to Study the Word

Hebrews 4:12 "For the word of God is living and active. Sharper than any double-edged sword, it penetrates even to dividing soul and spirit, joints and marrow; it judges the thoughts and attitudes of the heart."

...to Be Filled with Kindness and Joy

Jeremiah 31:3-4 "The Lord appeared to us in the past, saying: 'I have loved you with an everlasting love; I have drawn you with loving-kindness. I will build you up again and you will be rebuilt, O Virgin Israel. Again you will take up your tambourines and go out to dance with the joyful."

...to Follow the "Rules for Holy Living"

Colossians 3:5-8 "Put to death, therefore, whatever belongs to your earthly nature: sexual immorality, impurity, lust, evil desires and greed, which is idolatry. Because of these, the wrath of God is coming. You used to walk in these ways, in the life you once lived. But now you must rid yourselves of all such things as these: anger, rage, malice, slander, and filthy language from your lips."

Colossians 12-14 "Clothe yourselves with compassion, kindness, humility, gentleness and patience. Bear with each other and forgive whatever grievances you may have against one another. Forgive as the Lord forgave you. And over all these virtues put on love, which binds them all together in perfect unity."

...to Forgive

Matthew 18:21-22 "Then Peter came to Jesus and asked, 'Lord, how many times shall I forgive my brother when he sins against me? Up to seven times?' Jesus answered, 'I tell you, not seven times, but seventy-seven times.'"

...to Love

Psalm 17:6-8 "I call on you, O God, for you will answer me; give ear to me and hear my prayer. Show the wonder of your great love, you who save by your right hand those who take refuge in you from their foes. Keep me as the apple of your eye; hide me in the shadow of your wings."

...to Trust in God's Plan

Ecclesiastes 3:1-4 "There is a time for everything, and a season for every activity under heaven: a time to be born and a time to die, a time to plant and a time to uproot, a time to kill and a time to heal, a time to tear down and a time to build, a time to weep and a time to laugh."

...to Practice Humility

Galatians 6:3-5 "If anyone thinks he is something when he is nothing, he deceives himself. Each one should test his own actions. Then he can take pride in himself, without comparing himself to somebody else, for each one should carry his own load."

...to Apologize

2 Corinthians 7:10-11 "Godly sorrow brings repentance that leads to salvation and leaves no regret, but worldly sorrow brings death. See what this godly sorrow has produced in you: what earnestness, what eagerness to clear yourselves, what indignation, what alarm, what longing, what concern, what readiness to see justice done. At every point you have proved yourselves to be innocent in this matter."

...to Find Salvation

Exodus 15:2 "The Lord is my strength and my song; he has become my salvation. He is my God, and I will praise him, my father's God, and I will exalt him."

...to Stay Positive

Proverbs 15:13 "A happy heart makes the face cheerful, but heartache crushes the spirit."

...to Count Your Blessings

Ecclesiastes 5:19 "Moreover, when God gives any man wealth and possessions, and enables him to enjoy them, to accept his lot and be happy in his work—this is a gift of God."

...to Seek Strength in God's Love

Psalm 28:7 "The LORD is my strength and my shield; my heart trusts in him, and I am helped."

Build Confidence and Do Away with Jealous Feelings

Jealousy and insecurity are unattractive qualities that will drive a wedge between you and your spouse. Get control over jealous feelings by boosting your self-confidence. When you believe you are worthy of love, affection, and loyalty, your marriage is free to grow and mature as it should.

Categorize your accomplishments
Create a list all of your accomplishments within the past 5 years. Include items from the list below and add your own:

- Got an advanced degree
- Started a new job
- Received a promotion or a raise
- Received special commendation from a superior
- Honored with an award
- Started your own business
- Purchased a new home, car, etc.
- Paid down debt
- Paid off a loan or credit card
- Lost weight

- Stuck to an exercise program
- Changed diet for the better
- Became a parent
- Changed undesirable behaviors
- Told a hard truth
- Completed a physical challenge
- Traveled
- Finished a home-improvement project
- Overcame a fear
- Learned a new skill
- Increased your savings
- Invested wisely
- Took a risk

Acknowledge your strengths

People with low-self esteem work very hard to remind everyone of their faults. This behavior negatively reinforces low self-confidence, and must be stopped. Admit to at least 10 strengths from the list below—and add others not included—to switch focus from your faults to your strengths. Afterwards, ask yourself, "What's not to love?" Tell yourself you are:

- Honest
- Intelligent
- Funny
- Hard-working
- Loving
- Affectionate
- Thoughtful
- Adventurous
- Creative
- Driven
- Easy-going

- Motivated
- Trustworthy
- Trusting
- Devoted
- Spiritual
- Punctual
- Spontaneous
- Good listener
- Strong
- Dedicated
- Open minded

Marriage Retreats, Counseling & Other Support

Sometimes you need an unbiased third-party perspective to help you address and work through your marital issues. Be it a marriage and family counselor, a weekend retreat, or a series of marriage classes, speaking to a professional counselor or just sharing ideas with other couples who are in your same position can be immensely helpful and comforting. The following online resources, retreats, and other avenues of support can be useful in continuing to work at your marriage following this 40-day journey.

Marriage Retreats

If the spark in your marriage has gone out, or you're in need of time to reconnect, a marriage retreat may be helpful. You will find that many marriage retreats are Christian- or faith-based, although they welcome all non-denominational couples as well.

• **Retrouvaille:** This Catholic-based retreat is a series of presentations given by one of three couples and a priest that focus on specific areas of a marriage, followed by private reflection time given for each couple. Retrouvaille offers a series of post-weekend follow-up sessions to support couples after the initial retreat. Visit www.retrouvaille.org.

• **The National Marriage Encounter:** This Christian-based retreat offers weekend sessions focusing on enhancing communication for married or engaged couples. Marriage or Engaged Encounter weekends provide a safe environment for spouses to examine their lives together.
Visit www.marriages.org.

• **WinShape Marriage Retreats:** WinShape, created by the president of Chick-Fil-A, is a retreat for struggling couples or those looking to reconnect. They offer retreats for both engaged couples and married couples, everything from weekends away to a Caribbean sailing adventure. Visit www.winshape.org/marriage/programs.html.

Marriage Classes

If you are looking for more than a weekend, you might consider a series of ongoing marriage classes to learn techniques to improve communication and solidify your bond over time.

• **PREP (Prevention and Relationship Enhancement Program):** This program focuses on reducing "risk factors" and increasing "protective factors" to help marriages succeed. This program states it is not therapy, but education. Couples can attend public workshops ranging from Weekend Workshops, to 6 weekly sessions, to One-Day workshops taught by PREP Instructors. They also offer videotapes, audiotapes, and books for sale on their site. Visit www.prepinc.com.

• **PAIRS (Practical Application of Intimate Relationship Skills):** PAIRS hosts programs for couples in any stage of their relationship, varying in length from 1 day to 8 weeks to a semester. There are also programs in which your entire family can participate. Visit www.pairsfoundation.com.

Marriage Counseling

If you find that group settings are uncomfortable for you or your spouse, you should consider ongoing one-on-one sessions with a licensed marriage counselor.

• **Family and Marriage Counseling Directory:** This site offers a nationwide directory for counselors and therapists. Search by state and view daily articles on marriage and relationships. Visit http://family-marriage-counseling.com.

• **National Institute of Marriage:** The NIM conducts intensive Christian marriage counseling programs under the guidance of psychologists, marriage and family therapists, and licensed professional counselors.
Visit www.nationalmarriage.com/marriage_counseling.asp.

• **Center for Relational Care:** Providing faith-based counseling and workshops for couples, the Center also partners with churches, ministries, and other organizations around the world to provide a continuum of care for marriages, families, and individuals. Visit www.relationalcare.org.

Other Resources

• **The American Association for Marriage and Family Therapy** includes a printable "Consumer Guide to Marriage and Family Therapy," which lists "distress signals" to determine if you are in need of counseling, as well as questions to ask when interviewing a marriage therapist. Visit www.aamft.org/.

• **"The DNA of Relationships for Couples Marriage Conference":** A nationwide conference tour offered by the National Institute of Marriage. Visit www.nationalmarriage.com/marriage_conference.asp.

Write "The Story of Us"

Fill in the blanks in the story below to tell the tale of your relationship. Share the completed version with your spouse, and use it to open up a discussion about how your views of your relationship differ. Then share your expectations for how you can improve your relationship.

When I first met _____ I thought,

"_____!" But after just one date I

immediately knew that we were meant to _____.

Day and night I thought of his/her _____.

To this day, I still think about _____.

Our wedding day was the _____ day

of my life. Everything was _____.

I felt convinced that God put us together for a reason. And

that reason was to _____.

The first year of marriage was very _____.

My favorite thing about being married to him/her was _____

_____. Our conversations covered many topics

that have ranged from _____ to _____

_____. I continue to be impressed with the way my partner is

able to talk about _____.

Subsequent years brought about many changes, most of them

_____. For example, my partner started

to _____. I was surprised at first,

but I realized quickly that people change, so I handled it by

_____.

When I think about it, I've changed too. Now I am much more

_____ than I used to be. I think it makes

my partner feel _____. I would describe our

ability to communicate about these changes as _____

_____.

We've learned the hard way that marriage isn't easy. For example, I find it hard to cope when my partner _____ _____.

And of course, we have our arguments. In my honest opinion, most of them are _____fault. The things we fight over most include _____, _____ _____, and _____. These fights make me feel _____.

Over the years our sex life has _____. We have sex approximately _____ times a week, and I tend to _____ it. My sexual attraction to my spouse has _____ over the years. I would describe our sex life as _____.

One area in which I'd like to see our marriage improve is in the _____ department. I think if we fixed _____ we could be as happy as we were on the day we met. The best way I can think of to fix this problem is _____.

USE THE SPACE BELOW FOR OTHER

significant thoughts, emotions, or reflections:

_____

_____

_____

_____

_____

_____

_____

_____

_____

_____

_____

_____

_____

_____

_____

_____

_____

_____

_____

_____

Recommended Reading List

Cockrell, Stacie, et al. *Babyproofing Your Marriage: How to Laugh More and Argue Less as Your Family Grows*. New York: Collins Living, 2008.

Hanh, Thich Nhat. *Mindful Movements: Ten Exercises for Well-Being*. Berkeley, CA: Parallex Press, 2008.

Hunt, Mary. *Debt-Proof Your Marriage: How to Achieve Financial Harmony*. Ada, Michigan: Revell, 2004.

Landinsky, Daniel (translator). *Love Poems from God: Twelve Sacred Voices from East and West*. New York: Penguin, 2002.

Lluch, Alex. *Simple Principles for a Happy and Healthy Marriage*. San Diego: WS Publishing Group, 2008.

The Orthodox Study Bible: Ancient Christianity Speaks to Today's World. Nashville, TN: Thomas Nelson, 2008.

Read, Trina E. *Til Sex Do Us Part: Make Your Married Sex Irresistible*. Toronto, Ontario: Key Porter Books, 2008.

Skiff, Jennifer. *God Stories: Inspiring Encounters with the Divine*. New York: Three Rivers Press, 2009.

Warren, Rick. *Rick Warren's Bible Study Methods: Twelve Ways You Can Unlock God's Word*. New York: Harper Collins, 2006.

Conclusion

More than 2.2 million people say "I do," each year in the U.S.—
to the tune of an average of $20,398 per wedding. Weddings
are certainly big business and, as such, demand considerable
planning and effort. Indeed, women spend months trying on
dresses and auditioning florists, and couples visit numerous
locations and negotiate endlessly over fees, dates, and the
number of guests allowed. They taste dozens of wedding cakes
and potential meals to be served at the reception. The bride
and groom create several guest lists and separate them into
first, second, and third tiers so that no seat will go unfilled.
One or more years must be spent to plan a wedding, because
every little detail has to be perfect.

So much time, money, and energy is spent on this one-day
event. Yet the monumental effort a couple expends on putting
their wedding together often exceeds the work they put into
their marriages. In fact, when trouble arises in the relationship,
most couples claim they do not have time or money to do
what it takes to fix it. It is no wonder, then, that between 30
and 50 percent of all marriages end in divorce.

What sets you apart from other couples is that you chose to read and complete the exercises in *How God Can Save Your Marriage in 40 Days*. You made a commitment that was worth far more than the most expensive wedding. The work you put into the past 40 days was like taking out an insurance plan on your relationship that is backed by God. Indeed, you have learned that when you have faith in God's love and turn to His Word, anything is possible—even the resurrection of a relationship that felt like it was dead.

Hopefully, the exercises in *How God Can Save Your Marriage in 40 Days* made you feel more in control of your relationship. It taught you that commitment, communication, values, money, sex, joy, charity, and gratefulness are essential components of a happy and healthy marriage. You learned to use self-exploration to root out the ways in which you act contrary to God's wishes. As a result, you now understand that your thoughts, word, and actions have a significant impact on your relationship. You learned to accept responsibility for your contribution to marital problems and to forgive your spouse for his or her mistakes. This book taught you to give more than you thought yourself capable of to your spouse and to ask for nothing in return. And finally, you learned that the key to having a successful marriage is to model your love for your spouse after the way God loves you.

Journal

Use the following pages to reflect on your marriage and your 40-day journey. Note all the emotions, challenges, and successes experienced between you and your spouse as your relationship continues to grow. Revist these pages and witness the ways God's love strengthens your family and your marriage.

JOURNAL

_____

_____

_____

_____

_____

_____

_____

_____

_____

_____

_____

_____

_____

_____

_____

_____

_____

_____

_____

_____

_____

_____

_____

_____

_____

_____

_____

_____

_____

_____

_____

_____

_____

_____

_____

_____

_____

_____

_____

_____

_____

_____

_____

_____

JOURNAL